BELIEVING IN THE CROSS

Faith Is What You Have, Believing Is What You Do

REBECCA SIKES

Copyright © 2016 Rebecca Sikes.

All rights reserved. No part of this book may be used or reproduced by any means, graphic, electronic, or mechanical, including photocopying, recording, taping or by any information storage retrieval system without the written permission of the author except in the case of brief quotations embodied in critical articles and reviews.

Scripture taken from the Holy Bible, NEW INTERNATIONAL VERSION®. Copyright © 1973, 1978, 1984, 2011 by Biblica, Inc. All rights reserved worldwide. Used by permission. NEW INTERNATIONAL VERSION® and NIV® are registered trademarks of Biblica, Inc. Use of either trademark for the offering of goods or services requires the prior written consent of Biblica US, Inc.

WestBow Press books may be ordered through booksellers or by contacting:

WestBow Press
A Division of Thomas Nelson & Zondervan
1663 Liberty Drive
Bloomington, IN 47403
www.westbowpress.com
1 (866) 928-1240

Because of the dynamic nature of the Internet, any web addresses or links contained in this book may have changed since publication and may no longer be valid. The views expressed in this work are solely those of the author and do not necessarily reflect the views of the publisher, and the publisher hereby disclaims any responsibility for them.

Any people depicted in stock imagery provided by Thinkstock are models, and such images are being used for illustrative purposes only. Certain stock imagery © Thinkstock.

ISBN: 978-1-5127-2605-3 (sc)
ISBN: 978-1-5127-2607-7 (hc)
ISBN: 978-1-5127-2606-0 (e)

Library of Congress Control Number: 2016900140

Print information available on the last page.

WestBow Press rev. date: 01/20/2016

CHAPTER 1

Principles in Practice

Principles in practice—we all have something great inside of us. But we have to find out what it is and figure out how to make it best for us. The things one feels and believes on the inside are what matter most in life. I hope I can help you find the things you are searching for. That way you can be at peace—just like me.

You must develop a sound and committed relationship with our Father, the Lord Jesus Christ. He will be the one who will take care of you. He will protect you and guide you through all aspects of your life, good and bad.

Rebecca Sikes

+ his purpose
1. Christ
2. Family
3. Friends
4. Church

You must have priorities in life. Along with these priorities, you must think rationally and evaluate a plan for how to best deal with the trials and tribulations. Priorities are very important. They shape your decisions and your beliefs about how you feel, they inform the things that you cherish, and most of all, they are a major factor in the decisions you make throughout you entire life. Priorities will shape your life. They will shape your values (for better or worse), and they will inform your beliefs and ideas. But still most of all, your priorities will change your commitment to all aspects of things your heart, mind, and body engage in.

One of the most important lessons in life is to always do your best and try your hardest at everything—no matter what. You must have enthusiasm, energy, and most of all, the motivation to see projects to their very end. You must do what you can to tap into all of your available resources to make this happen. You must always strive to improve and get better. Try to stir up the dream that is in your heart. Even though it may just be a dream, it can be attainable.

As people grow and change their priorities, their visions for the future seem to also change. We expect wealth, recognition, happiness, perfection, and most of all, peace. In this ever-changing world, we all must reevaluate our priorities, what we think about, how we spend our money, and how we spend our time. We must decide if we are providing a service to the ones in need. We need to share what we have in knowledge and wisdom about the things that sometimes make us stumble. It is the simple things like this that most people do not realize can change the world around them. You must have faith. When faith comes, you will have solitude. You will feel its presence. It will come in the form of glory and grace. Our acceptance is an act of faith. Faith is a response to the call.

Believing in the Cross

Faith alone will justify how we feel and what paths we will take in our lives. The Disciples of Christ followed the Father through their trials and tribulations. This was their form of acceptance and their ongoing relationship with Christ. God will continue to perfect the attributes you possess. These changes will take place over time as your faith continues to grow and become stronger.

> And every one who calls on the name of the Lord
> will be saved. (Acts 2:21)

Passion is a feeling of intense love toward a certain individual or entity. Passion will grow through Christ. It will deepen relationships. It may also form unique personal relationships.

To have happiness, we must believe in Christ. Happiness comes from faith and the unseen things in life. Even though we know the journey may be long, we will follow the one who went before us. We must give Christ our minds, hearts, and souls. We must continue to be obedient and have discipline. Individuals must deepen their roots in their faith in Jesus Christ. Christianity must become the core of all values and beliefs. The toughest decisions are made easier with faith in Jesus Christ.

People with faith who are seeking understanding will be informed of the truth, which will come in the form of the word of the Bible. You will find good news when you seek and understand the truth. God will put people in our path who have the knowledge and understanding of faith.

> I love those who love me; and those who seek me
> find me. (Proverbs 8:17)

The Lord tells us that if we seek him, we will find him.

Wisdom is a wonderful discernment. It has so many endless abilities. Every individual needs to have wisdom for making decisions. You are not born with wisdom, and neither is it given to you. Wisdom is gathered throughout life with the decisions that are made and the events that shape our lives. To recognize what you need, you must first know yourself spiritually, mentally, and physically. And you must study Scripture to grow spiritually and mentally. An individual can always ask for God's help to figure out what he or she needs to study in order to grow. Through study and obedience we can grow through grace. An attempt to follow God's ways and his Word is always comprised of thoughts of peace. Put all of your effort in giving Christ your mind and heart in study so you can be transformed into the unique and authentic person he wants you to be. We can show growth in our individual situations because the Holy Spirit wants us to know that what is within the reach of one is also well within the reach of others.

In the eyes of Christ, we should not feel isolated. We must get out and do the things we were created to do on this earth. One of the most important things you can do is smile at people. Let them know you are influenced by Christ. We can offer emotional support to people who need it. Sometimes people just need a voice to tell them it will be okay. Other times people just need a laugh or hug to make them feel like there is nothing they can't do or succeed at. When you sacrifice yourself for the good of others, you show the love in your heart. This will give people the confidence and power to overcome all challenges.

By grace we are awakened. We are opened up to the gifts and thoughts of the Lord as well as what path he wants us to follow. We also have a spiritual gift that is given to us by the Lord. This gift will allow us to follow the message and embrace the attributes given to us by our Father. When you receive the Holy Spirit, you will receive the fruit of the Spirit. Love, joy, peace, patience, kindness, generosity, faithfulness, loyalty, gentleness, and self-control are all fruits of the Holy Spirit.

Love. This is a feeling of the heart and soul toward someone or something, and it cannot be broken. This is an emotion that allows that loved person to be placed entirely at the top of all priorities and needs above yourself.

Joy. This is a feeling of complete happiness with your life and surroundings. Joy will allow you to be happy with yourself and with others so you can see the good in all things and all people.

Peace. Peace is an emotion that allows you to sit back and relax, knowing you have been put on this earth with a purpose. If you are at peace with yourself, you are at peace with God. Having peace will allow you to know that you have done all you can to help people in need and to change the things you are able to change. This feeling allows us to know we are following the Lord's plan and doing what he asks us to do.

Patience. This is an emotion that will allow us to wait for good things to happen. Patience also gives us the strength to help others in need and to know their fortunes will soon turn out well. No one knows how much patience we must have. Every situation and person is different. We just cannot give up on anyone or anything. We must know that sooner or later, with patience and trust in the Lord, goodness will prevail.

Kindness. This feeling is often overlooked. We often get so wrapped up in what is going on around us that we forget about

5

the simplest things. Kindness to others shows them that there are people out there who care. Kindness is sometimes just as simple as a smile, a polite hello, or a nice compliment. It can instantly change the way people feel about themselves or can just brighten their day. The golden rule tells you to always be nice, since you should want for others the same things you want for yourself.

Generosity. Others always appreciate this. People always need help. Most people do not ask for it for fear of imposing on others. They may feel embarrassed about the situation. Always help others, as sooner or later, you will need that same help from others. Give your fruits and possessions to people in need. When you give to others, you will be overcome with a feeling of bliss and relief, knowing you helped someone through whatever he or she needed in life.

Faithfulness and loyalty. These two can be put together as one. When you are faithful and loyal, you hold a person or entity as the highest point in your life. Being faithful and loyal to God, your family, and your friends will give you a feeling of love and trust. As God is your spine, your family and friends are your ribs. Faithfulness and loyalty will allow these relationships to come together as one.

Gentleness. Some may call this compassion. This is needed a lot more than is realized. Gentleness can be given when someone is sick, hurt, or just going through a rough time. Gentleness will let people know that you truly care.

Self-control. This is often the hardest and most confusing emotion we can have. Sometimes we do or say things we shouldn't. And when we do or say these types of things, people can become offended and have their feelings hurt. We all have a path to follow in this life. Stay on the right track, follow what the Lord has asked you to do, and always think before acting out.

Believing in the Cross

If the things listed above are what you seek, you must develop these essentials for an abundant life. These come from the Holy Spirit. They can only develop through the Spirit and can only be led by the Spirit. By following these essentials, our lives will be holy, and our salvation will be secure.

We all need to change situations that need to be changed. Where we stand on situations determines how we see them. Human reality determines where we stand. This discipline is identifies who is in need without concern. God will put these situations in your path. He will let you decide how to deal with them. You must be grateful that he has the confidence and trust in you to do the right thing. When you involve yourself in Christian actions, you are doing God's work.

The person to whom we choose to listen determines what we hear and our faith in Christianity. Joy is a contagious emotion when you are able to fully accept being a Christian. Action is a grateful response to God's grace in all who believe in Christ.

There are many obstacles to grace. If you choose the actions of yourself only, you must practice the presence of God as you will gain the feeling of mercy. Ask the Lord if there is any wicked way in you. Anything that can keep us from a relationship with God can be a sin. It will make you the center of sin. In some cases you can consider it to be alienating yourself from God and his works. If you disobey the signs of the Lord that are set in front of you, you will miss the path he has set forth for you and your life.

For Christians, the Bible is our standard for the studies and teachings of God. Diverging from this book and the teachings of God can hinder our relationship with God and other relationships throughout the course of our everyday life. Obstacles we come across can be anything that will keep us from God's grace.

We should always be reconciled with our neighbors. In this practice, we must forgive our brothers, our sisters, and even our enemies. Forgiveness is the basis of all of God's commands. Without forgiveness in your heart, you will always be left with a feeling of remorse.

You have to belong to the body of Christ. When you have accepted Christ in your life, your soul will open up and have a feeling of completeness. You will feel love for everyone, including your enemies, and most of all, you will feel love and compassion for yourself. Good self-esteem is one of the most important things to have in life. When you have a good feeling about yourself, you can be happy with everyone and everything around you. Try to participate in all means of grace, including love, laughter, thoughtfulness, kindness, and self-control. Always try to be positive about the things you cannot change. These attributes will help you live a happy and prosperous life.

Practice works of mercy, whether they be in your heart or physically helping others. There will always be more grace in God than there will be sin in us. Come open the door, and let God in. All you have to do is ask. He will always answer your needs in some way. You may not see it or understand what he is doing, but he knows. This will be the path he has set for you. Through God's grace, we are able to find new blessings each and every day. Ask to have mercy. There are always sins that live below the surface. These are hidden and may never be realized by anyone. God knows they are there, and you must remove these from your heart and mind, as that is what he wants and needs. *Help me, Lord.*

Believing in the Cross

> You, dear children, are from God and have overcome Them, because the one who is in you is greater than the one who is in the world. (1 John 4:4)

One of the most important parts of being a Christian is being in a discipleship with God. A disciple is a growing person who is probably in all of us. It is a minister, a full-time Christian, a witness to Christ, and also a Christian leader. A disciple knows his or her priorities. This person has discipline. He or she knows reality and how to overcome all it has to offer. This person will show empathy toward others and also takes initiative when needed. Disciples are also very generous with everything that they possess, mentally, physically, and spiritually. Disciples are Christ's leaders. They will save the people of the world, follow Jesus, and feed his sheep. They put their faith into action and believe in Jesus. You know by their actions that they are very special people. One must realize that God always has the right people in the right place at the right time. This is his choice and his vision for you. A disciple takes initiative, seeing every opportunity through to the end. By taking initiatives, the Acts of the Apostles will continue through us. A disciple is a generous person; he or she is blessed and full of spiritual qualities. He or she is a disciple of Jesus Christ, you too can be one also.

You have to have faith. You have to have the motivation that God can do and accomplish anything. Always have hope; through God everything is possible. You must have love. You will realize that every person matters. Through this we can share the good things in life with everyone. You can change the world by piety, devoutness, the study of the Word, and most of all your actions. Always walk in the light of God. Have justice for your community and the world.

Be kind to others, and you must have a plan for anchoring yourself. We change our hearts through piety, our minds through study, and our bodies through action. We are all called to love and have mercy for other people.

> He man who loves his life will lose it, while the man who hates his life in this world will keep it for eternal life. Whoever served me must follow me; and where I am, my servant also will be. My Father will honor the one who serves me. (John 12:25–26)

You must follow Christ the Father and only him. It is an honor and a privilege. Make an inventory of your relationships. Your attitude will make all the difference in everything you do or come across. Always have the golden rule in mind.

> So in everything, do to others what you would have them do to you, for this sums up the law and the prophets. (Matthew 7:12)

This principle of action and mode of life is in fact the sum of all Bible teachings. Through prayer you make people change. Make sure your ministry changes people. Make a friend, be a friend, and most of all, send a friend to be reunited with Christ. *Christ does us for this – it is not us.*

> Therefore go and make disciples of all nations, baptizing them in the name of the Father and of the Son and of the Holy Spirit. And teaching them to obey everything I have commanded you. And

** *Not sure we can make people change, but Christ can.*

surely I am with you always till the very end of the age. (Matthew 28:19–20)

This is a promise of God. He will follow you and help you in your endeavors. He will lead you in your challenge, giving you the support and direction you will need to fulfill your conquests and endeavors. Feel it in your heart and in your mind, and do it in your actions. You must have faith.

To spread the Word of God, you must have a plan. Some will plant the seed of God, some will water the seed, and some will harvest the crop. You must decide which action you will take. God will follow you every step of the way. Be a disciple for Christ. That is what he has chosen for us to be.

Let us discuss grace. How about sanctifying grace? It is the work of the Holy Spirit. What God has done for us is sanctification.

> And we know that in all things God works for good of those who love him, who have been called according to his purpose. (Romans 8:28)

It means his purpose, and he is the one who knows the plan that makes all possible. Find ways to give more. Your life is a journey; enjoy it to the fullest, for it only lasts a short time. Sanctifying grace is a gift. You have to strengthen your grace. There are lot of ways this can be done throughout life. The workings of the Holy Spirit provide the power to work God's grace. It is always active in every good deed. Some important things to remember are love and action. Our response to the things we do in God's teachings should be love and action. When we want to change for the better, this is God acting in our life, showing us the love and devotion to change the things in our lives. Sanctifying grace is to be obedient and to have divine energy. We have to transform our hearts. Sanctifying grace is an amazing thing. It equips us to see how great the Holy Spirit really is. It also shows us what the Holy Spirit can do in our lives.

> For you did not receive a spirit that makes you a slave again to fear, but you received the spirit of son ship. And by him we cry, "ABBA," Father. The Spirit himself testifies with our spirit that we are Gods children. Now if we are children, then we are heirs-heirs of God and co-heirs with Christ, if indeed we share in his sufferings in order that we may also share in his glory. (Romans 8:15–17)

We should glorify him. He has made it possible for us all to live in his grace. This aspect can be thought of as restoring our lives like an old chair. You have the photo of the before, and then you have the photo of what it looks like after a total cleansing and acceptance of our Holy Father. The need to restore our lives should be felt by all. It should be a natural emotion and response to our Father, Jesus Christ.

We should be perfecting our daily routines. It is said that we should impart ourselves to other people. We must open our hearts up and share the important events in all of our lives. One act should be to equip ourselves with the fruits of the Spirit. Being justified by faith gives us the chance that we should give other people—a chance of sanctification experiences in his grace. Experience a change of heart versus a change of status.

Believing in the Cross

> Since we have now been justified by his blood, how much more shall we be saved from God's wrath through him. (Romans 5:9)

In our holy communion, we experience perfecting ourselves and becoming mature Christians. The love and the fruits of the spirit all come alive when we feel God's presence in our hearts and souls. While perfecting ourselves, every vine and branch in our hearts, our souls, and our minds will be pruned. You will be perfected in love and faith.

As we grow older, we are supposed to reach a stage when we become more mature. At each stage the believer will become more comfortable in areas of his or her life. Believers will be able to decide what choices are to be made over right and wrong. They will also learn how to put the needs of others ahead of their own.

> I am the true vine, and my Father is the gardener. He cuts off every branch in me that bears no fruit, while every branch that does bear fruit he prunes so it will be even more fruitful. (John 15:1–2)

We must maintain that faith. Very strong faith can get us through any situation. If we lose that faith, the momentum is lost. We must always have this faith in our Lord. Remember to always remind yourself that he will never put more on a person than he or she can handle. As you grow in Christ, the joy of his salvation will come. Along with this, peace will venture into your heart and soul. He wants this for us. This is what he has chosen for us. The least we can do daily is to reach up to our Lord, Jesus Christ, with faith and

13

love in our hearts for him. God loves us so much, and he has given us the power to overcome all things blocking our paths.

> And hope does not disappoint us, because God has poured out his love into our hearts by the Holy Spirit, whom he has given us. (Romans 5:5)

Pray for the Holy Spirit with all you have. He wants a relationship with all his sheep. All you have to do is ask and come to him with an open heart. A total commitment in your heart and soul is all he begs of you. Pray with fire in your spirit and desire in your heart. We cannot help ourselves; we need God's help daily in our thoughts, prayers, and souls to secure the foundation that is to be given to us.

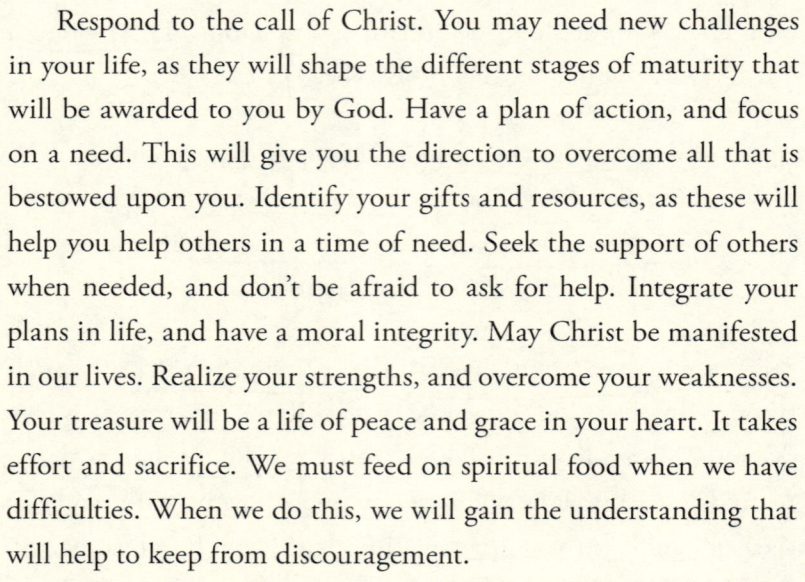

Respond to the call of Christ. You may need new challenges in your life, as they will shape the different stages of maturity that will be awarded to you by God. Have a plan of action, and focus on a need. This will give you the direction to overcome all that is bestowed upon you. Identify your gifts and resources, as these will help you help others in a time of need. Seek the support of others when needed, and don't be afraid to ask for help. Integrate your plans in life, and have a moral integrity. May Christ be manifested in our lives. Realize your strengths, and overcome your weaknesses. Your treasure will be a life of peace and grace in your heart. It takes effort and sacrifice. We must feed on spiritual food when we have difficulties. When we do this, we will gain the understanding that will help to keep from discouragement.

Continue to have passion. Do not let the world take it from you. The flesh has a way of taking this from our hearts. Always believe in yourself. Always believe you are special and were put on this earth with a divine purpose. Stay focused. Stay in touch with Christ and most of all with the people God has given you to influence. Grace has not been given to you to store and lock up. Share it with others and believe in others, and so they will believe in you also. God's love will follow you wherever you go. These are the things that can and will shape our lives and make us the person God intended us to be.

CHAPTER 2

THE DARKNESS IN YOUR LIFE

This chapter will hopefully help you address the elephant in the room. Are you ready for this? If you can relate to any of the acts listed here or maybe even have done them yourself, they are sin. In this chapter we will discuss the Ten Commandments, which are listed in Exodus in the Bible. We will also lightly touch on some other things that may not be considered sins but are not right in the eyes of the father. Gossip, slander, dishonor, disobedience, unbelief, ignorance, pride, and unforgiving are all sins that are created by the evil that lives inside us.

1. "You shall have no other gods before me." God should always at the top of our lives. He is the only one we should ever view as the Holy One. The manner in which this first commandment is given tells us that each individual of the nation is addressed individually and is required solely as one to obey the law, a mere general obedience being less than acceptable; this commandment requires the worship of one God alone. It implies that there is no other God.
2. "You shall not make for yourself an idol in the form of anything in heaven above, on the earth beneath, or in the waters below. You shall not bow down to them, or worship them; for I, the Lord, your God, am a jealous God, punishing the children for the sin of the fathers to the third and fourth generation of those who hate me, but showing love to a thousand generations of those who love me and keep my commandments." Those who ignore this commandment are guilty of the sin of idolatry.
3. "You shall not misuse the name of the Lord, your God, in vain; for the Lord will not hold anyone guiltless who misuses his name." Taking the name of the Lord in vain consists of all swearing and disrespect of his name in everyday life.
4. "Remember the Sabbath day, by keeping it holy. Six days you shall labor, and do all your work, but the seventh days is a Sabbath to the Lord your God. On it you shall not do any work, neither you, nor your son, nor your daughter, nor your man servant, nor your maid servant, nor your animals, nor the alien that is within your gates. For in six days the Lord made the heavens, the earth, the sea, and all that is in them, but he rested the seventh day. Therefore the Lord

blessed the Sabbath day and made it holy." The seventh day was not so much to be a day of worship, as we think of it now, but rather a day of rest. Even the very beasts that are used every day should be given the opportunity of rest. All were to observe this day. The Sabbath was no exception. It was meant to portray the fact that there is rest in Christ, as we must also have rest in our hearts, as the heavenly Father would want us to observe.

5. "Honor your father and your mother, so that you may live long in the land the Lord your God has given you." Honoring your father and mother is the basis of honoring God; the first few of these commandments have to do with our relationship with God, while the latter have to do with relationships with fellow man.

6. "You shall not murder." God, in his Holy Word, commands high-ranking officials to put evil men to death, which is known as execution. This is not murder; murder and execution are two different actions used in different ways.

7. "You shall not commit adultery." This is a sin that must be observed by both man and woman. In the Lord's eyes husbands and wives are considered one and in the same flesh. This is a bond that should never be broken once the sacramental union has been taken. This union should never be treated as anything else and should always be viewed as a union of love, of trust, and of the heart.

8. "You shall not steal." We simply do not take that which does not belong to us. It is a matter of integrity and respect. If it is not yours, respect it as someone else's and honor that.

9. "You should not give false testimony against your neighbor." We should honor the relationships we have with other people. We shall not tell untruths about our neighbors or slander their names falsely in public or in private.
10. "You shall not covet your neighbors' house. You shall not covet your neighbors' wife, or his man servant, or his maid servant, his ox, or donkey, or anything that belongs to your neighbor." In life we should not envy what our neighbor has. There is always someone who will have and acquire better things than others. Always remember that the Lord will provide to us what we need. All other things are of the material and have no bearing on our life with our Lord Jesus Christ. (Exodus 20:3-17)

The Ten Commandments given by God to Moses on Mt. Sinai are the foundation of all law, at least law that is righteous, for the entire world; it is the moral law of God and as such, cannot change. Here is a list of other items that may not be sins of the Lord but may be considered sins of the personal well-being inside of us that will cause separation from God.

1. Dishonor: To bring insult or disgrace to another person or thing.
2. Ignoring: To intentionally disregard or dismiss.
3. Obedience: Refusing to obey individuals or laws that are set forth.
4. Disbelief: Refusal to believe the truth.
5. Pride: An undue sense of superiority and personal dignity.
6. Unforgiveness: The balance or feeling of resentment against another person.

Let us go in to detail on a couple of other things that are not sins of the Lord but are sins that are of the inner- self that is always inside of us.

Let's mention lying here. This is sometimes done to cover up things that are done or that are done by a person who has done something wrong. This will always have negative consequences when the truth comes out. People always get hurt emotionally. Sometimes a relationship is destroyed and may be unrecoverable. It can destroy many of the good things that exist in life. God wants you to always tell the truth to everyone. If the truth can be told, forgiveness is almost always going to happen. Always look to God for help. He can give you the courage to tell the truth.

Gossip is when you have nothing to say about someone or something that has any meaning or purpose. It is usually done when a person is not there or able to defend him or herself. It may be about something that person has done or may be doing at the moment. This has no purpose and usually has an emotional effect on the person who is being talked about. It only makes the person who is leading and the ones involved in the conversation look like the fools. Often they do not know what has really happened, and it is usually far from the truth. I guess the rule that we should live by is, "If you don't have anything nice to say, it is usually better of left unsaid."

Slander is making false statements or misrepresentations to injure or defame someone or something. These statements have no purpose. Slanderous statements are forbidden in the eyes of God. He is always judging and always wanting us to do the right thing by our brothers and sisters. Slanderous statements are mostly untrue even though they may have a close relation to the subject at hand.

Always speak the truth about other people as you would like them to do the same thing for you.

Sin is going to exist no matter what. Whether it is ourselves or someone else, we must develop a way to properly handle it. All people have sin in their lives.

> But he who sins against me wrongs his own soul: all they who hate me love death. (Proverbs 8:36)

> Behold, all souls are mine; as the soul of the father, so also the soul of the son is mine: the soul that sins, it shall die. (Ezekiel 18:14)

To become recognized by our neighbors and belong to the body of Christ, we must begin to know and love ourselves. We should participate in all the means of grace, pray for our leaders, and practice works of mercy. Practice these things, and you will be at peace, as God always wants for his children. There is always much more grace in God than there is sin in us. If you have sin in your life, here is a short prayer to help you out:

> Dear Lord Jesus I now realize that I am a sinner. I accept the fact that you died for me on that rugged cross of Calvary. I now open my heart's door and receive you as the Savior and Lord of my life. Please take full control and help me to be the kind of Christian you need me to be. Amen.

You must realize that when Satan was cast out of heaven, so were one-third of the angels. Open your eyes to what is going on around you, whether it be with you neighbors, your friends, your enemies, or events that are changing the world. Many of these things will have adverse actions on you and everything around you. Be cautious and knowledgeable.

God says that his people perished because of a lack of knowledge. Sin starts because of one bad thought. Every bad thought comes from Satan; every good thought is said to come from God.

> He replied, "I saw Satan fall like lightning from Heaven." (Luke 10:18)

Satan tortures the demons if they do not do what he says, and you must realize that he will torture you also.

Satan is real. Even though you may not be able to see him, he is alive and out there trying to find a weakness in someone to manifest himself in. It is a thought and belief that people who are condemned to hell will get a different body. That body will be in pain all of the time, always aching and hurting for the Father to save him or her. You will always feel pain and suffering and sorrow. If that is not enough for you to believe in the Father, the thought of your flesh burning off and the pain of fire should make you believe in Christ.

> There was a rich man who was dressed in purple and fine linen and lived in luxury every day. At his gate was laid a beggar named Lazarus covered with sores. And longing to eat what fell from the rich man's table. Even the dogs came and licked his sores. The time came when the beggar died and the angels carried him to Abraham's side. The rich man also died and was buried. In hell, where he was In

> torment, he looked up and saw Abraham far away,
> with Lazarus by his side. So he called to him, Father
> Abraham have pitty on me and send Lazarus to dip
> the tip of his finger in water and cool my tongue,
> because I am in agony in this fire. (Luke 16:19-24)

This is the sentence that he was given by God for the sins he had done.

> The thief comes only to steal and kill and destroy;
> I have come that they may have life, and have it to
> the full. (John 10:10)

Let us break this all down. You need to understand it completely. Satan is the thief who steals your salvation. He kills the people you love. He can also destroy your life or anyone in your family's life before you even realize it. You must prevent this from happening. Stay involved in the lives of the people you care about. Always be concerned by the slightest thing that is out of order. Always be there to help them in the time of need. They may not ask for help, but you will know when they need it. Pray every day to have the life that Jesus offers to you. Have the faith of a Christian. Always remember that God will test your faith. Satan will tempt your actions with sin.

> Put on the full armor of God so that you can take
> your stand against the devils schemes. (Ephesians
> 6:11)

Satan uses people to come up against us. We must pay attention to our youth. They are the ones who are the most fragile. Many youth are not able to find their purpose or make the right decisions to shape their lives in the right way. The suicide rate in teens is at an all-time high. We as adults are obligated to follow and help them make the right decisions. If you see a youth struggling or dealing with enormous problems, you must act to save him or her. It is your job as a Christian. Youth do not have the knowledge and courage to seek help for themselves. We must take the initiative to help them or at least find them the help they deserve.

As an adult, if you are having problems, find someone to talk to. Do not let it manifest into something you cannot control. Jesus Christ is the healer in all of us.

> The tongue has the power of life and death, and
> those who love it will eat its fruit. (Proverbs 18:21)

If you speak evil, you will reap evil. Speak good things so good will come to you. Be careful—Satan is very patient. He will wait. He will seek out the ones he can devour. What Satan means for harm, God will turn it around and use it for his glory. Demons are very powerful. They compel us to destroy our lives. One way to look at it is fighting an invisible war. We have to keep discussing it. How would you know the positive things if you did not first know the negative things? If you have Christ in your heart, you have already won the battle. Just keep pushing forward and keep the faith of the Father. There is no pessimism going on here; this is happening. We must have a rich knowledge of what is going on around us at all times.

Sometimes we get overwhelmed with emotion. Our emotions can only be settled by the Holy Spirit. Our faith gives Satan no place in our hearts. In some way or another Satan has us in bondage. His ways are very deceptive. We say, "I love God," and then we sin in some form. We say, "I love God," and then we sin again.

> In your anger do not sin. Do not let the sun go down while you are still angry, and do not give the devil a foothold. (Ephesians 4:26–27)

The only anger allowed is righteous anger. All other anger is a result of the "old man" and must be put off.

> A gentle answer turns away wrath, but a harsh word stirs up danger. (Proverbs 15:1)

Even one grievous word against another stirs up anger. Any discussion that becomes heated instantly becomes an uncontrollable discussion, which will only lead to more wrath. We cause this type of anger ourselves. Only when the self is hidden in Christ can we properly emphasize self-discipline.

> Therefore put on the full armor of God, so that when the day of evil comes, you may be able to stand your ground, and after you have done everything to stand. [This may be interpreted as the reason we face resisting and opposing the power of darkness. This may refer to the believer not giving up ground.] Stand firm then, with the belt of truth buckled around your waist, with the breastplate of righteousness in place. [This may be interpreted as the truth of Christ and the righteousness of Christ, which comes by way of the cross.] And with your

feet fitted with the readiness that comes from the gospel of peace. [This may interpreted as that peace comes to you by way of the cross as well.] In addition to all this, take up the shield of faith, with which you can extinguish all the flaming arrows of the evil one. [This may be interpreted as making Christ the object of your faith, which is the only faith God will recognize. This is the only faith Satan will recognize as well. This represents temptations Satan will give to all of us.] Take the helmet of salvation and sword of the spirit, which is in the word of God. [This may also be interpreted as having to do with the place of our minds. We must realize God is everything—the creation, time, and us. He did everything through the cross and its idealistic state.] (Ephesians 6:13–17)

The believer must not give Satan a single inch. You must renew your mind. Remember that God is always in your heart, and always remember that Satan will come to you through your mind and thoughts. That is so important to remember if you get angry or argue with someone who has been introduced into your heart by Satan. Sit back and remind yourself that Satan is putting these actions and thoughts into your mind. He will never give up. You must always be ready and able to defend yourself from these actions. Please spread the word of Christ. People don't understand sometimes that families that have problems may not realize what is happening. Make them realize, and comfort them. Save them from more hurt and more tears. We must save God's children. We are of flesh and blood. The

Enemy is an evil entity that can destroy all if we allow it to happen. Satan puts detours in our lives to throw us off course so we will not focus on the things that are most important. Satan represents death; Jesus represents life. Please arm yourself and be ready to defend yourself against the actions sent forth by Satan.

We are going to move on to a topic that we can all relate to. You will be astonished by this.

People who talk doubt, talk death. People who speak the word of God speak of life. Our words are so important. We all do it; we are all humans, but stop and think about what you say. Remember: in the beginning of time God uttered very powerful words during his creation of life.

> And God said, "Let there be light, and there was light." (Genesis 1:3)

"God said." He spoke this into existence. You are saying it, believing it, and it is happening. I hope you understand the quote of "God said," when we say something, it is so very important, not only for you or to the person you are talking to, but also God hears you. Be careful what you say. You must always remember what and how you say something to someone. God is always listening.

> Dear friends, do not believe every spirit, but test the spirits to see whether they are from God, because many false prophets have gone out into the world. This how you can recognize the Spirit of God: every spirit that acknowledges that Jesus Christ has come in the flesh is from God. But every spirit that does not acknowledge Jesus is not from God. This is

the spirit of the antichrist, which you have heard
is coming and even now is already in the world.
(John 4:1–3)

You have to ask yourself, did this come in the name of Jesus? God is not confusion. You can tell the difference. Remember: everything good comes from God, and everything bad comes from Satan. This pertains to all objects and experiences. God is greater that Satan; he is the Word. It is up to you to be able to tell the difference. Satan employs seducing spirits. God is good all the time. There are things that God does not like. I have listed a few examples that are of my personal preference: a proud look, a lying tongue, murder (hands that shed innocent blood), a wicked heart, feet that are swift and run to mischief (pay back), a false witness that spreads gossip and lies, and one who sows discord among the brethren. I don't know about you, but I am guilty of doing these all of the time. We have to pay attention to what we are doing and saying. These mistakes will in the end come back to haunt us, possibly for the rest of our lives. We're not perfect, but we can work toward becoming better Christians, living for God, and making God first in our lives. Faith comes by hearing, and hearing comes from listening to the Word of God. Hearing is studying the Word of God and being involved in your place of worship. It may be in a church or even at home as long as you are studying the Word of God.

> Jesus said, "If the world hates you, keep in mind
> that it hated me first." (John15:18)

People like living in sin. You have to draw the line in the sand. You must always stay on the right side—the side of God. It says to study and make ourselves worthy. In the end of times, God will pour out his Spirit. God will reveal things that we do not know. Salvation is a gift. The Holy Spirit is also a gift given by God. What Satan means for harm, God will turn around for his glory. There is life after death, to be present from the body is to be present with the Lord.

> And the devil said to him, "If you be the son of God, tell this stone to become bread." (Luke 4:3)

The Devil tempted Jesus over and over.

A lesson on the Devil is that Satan is a fallen angel who led a revolution against God in eternity past. He was one of the most powerful angels ever created by God. He served God in righteousness and holiness for an undetermined period of time before his fall from grace. Satan gained authority because of the default of Adam and Eve.

When we pray, we must try to say, "Lord, you know what it will take." We should not say whatever it takes, leaving to door wide open for Satan to come in and do "whatever" it takes. Some believe that Satan has access to heaven. He is the accuser of people. Jesus is our adversary. When Satan accuses us of bad things, Jesus says, "No, forgive them." Remember when Jesus was on the cross,

> Jesus said, "Father, forgive them, they know not what they are doing."(Luke 23:34)

We must pray about this often.

There are certain things that disrupt a normal life. Pride, envy, and jealousy are some of the most misunderstood, and they sometimes also do the most damage.

Pride causes people not to be believers in God. It causes people to think they do not need any help with anything or even help from others. This is so untrue. We all need God and everything associated with him, especially with what happened on the cross. He had no pride in giving himself so we could survive and prosper.

Envy is a painful and resentful awareness of an advantage enjoyed by another. Envy wants to have what someone else possesses. Envy may be sneaky. It may be subtle. Envy is forever reaching and longing for us to say or think sinister insinuations.

> For jealousy arouses a husbands fury, and he will show no mercy when he takes revenge. (Proverbs 6:34)

Jealousy is coarse and cruel. It clothes and smothers you. It causes people to do things without thinking. When you are jealous of something or someone, you will do whatever you can to eliminate whatever is bothering you. In most cases people snap and make decisions they later regret.

> See if there is any offensive way in me and lead me in the way everlasting. (Psalm 139:24)

This refers to Jesus, and he is perfect. Unfortunately, we are not. You really have to reach deep into your heart and search Jesus out. This is what Satan does best; he puts obstacles in front of us to try to get us off course in our lives. It hinders our relationship with

God. He tries to alienate us from God. Flesh and blood will always be tempted and tainted by sin. We must do everything we can to use our hearts and minds in a good way that will follow the works of Christ. It is better to endure harm than to lose one's soul. You have to suffer; nothing should come easy. If you are one of the lucky ones for whom it does come easy, enjoy it, but remember, there may be price to pay in the end.

Trials are tests. They are there for you to learn from your mistakes. Correct them and move on, but remember to always learn from them and find ways to avoid making the same ones over and over again. We all must go through bad times and the consequences of the mistakes we have made. This is how we get stronger and grow in our lives. Our emotions play a big role in our lives. They have control over everything we do. We must get control of our emotions before we can make rational decisions.

Anger is a very strong emotion. It is everywhere. You must always remember who is behind this. He is always lurking and waiting to jump at any chance to play on this emotion in your mind and heart. The Bible tells us to be slow to anger. Most people are not. They will say and do things that result in nothing positive. Sometimes people get hurt or even killed. This emotion has no place in your heart. Remember: with anger, nobody wins. Here is something to remember: if a person gets angry, it is not the person; it is the spirit in the person. You should not blame that person. He or she knows that his or her actions or words were wrong. That person now has deal with it. There are consequences for our choices. We are what we speak. The things that we hate are most of the things we do without realizing it.

Believing in the Cross

This is for the believer. Say, "I bind you, Satan. That same thing is also bound in heaven." When you lose something on earth, it shall be lost in heaven. Bind up all your weakness.

> I tell you the truth, whatever you bind on earth will be bound in heaven and whatever you loose on earth will loosed in heaven. (Matthew 18:18)

Disobeying God will put a block in between the two of you. You must walk with the Lord and must have obedience while doing it. We must realize what is happening around us. Today, more than ever, there is a spiritual warfare happening. There are demon spirits trying to get us into bondage and causing quarrels and conflicts between all humankind. They will bring trouble, sorrow, and even death for us all. Sinners are in darkness, and some of them do not know what to do to avoid the possibility of being dragged into a deep downward spiral caused by the worldly situations. They will act out toward their brothers and sisters in Christ. Then these people will undoubtedly have regret and shame for their actions. We are capable of solving these things, but the attacks will still occur. We as individuals can overcome this if we find a way to come to grips with reality. We must walk with God and understand what happened on the cross. When in doubt, you must ask God for mercy, and honor God with your life. Realize that God owns everything. He created it all, and he can take it all away. Realize in your heart and mind that you are fighting a war that has already been won for each and every one of us. Remember that if God is for you, who can be against you? If it is not of faith, it is of sin. We must be careful with our words.

If you talk doubt, you will be talking death. You can never be negative. If you have a negative or bad attitude, this is your inner enemy. You must change how you feel and see situations as they are. It will only make you feel better as a person and as a brother of Christ. Ask God to go before you. You must put on all of your armor. Don't be self-indulgent. If you are a glutton, that is not good. Remember that gluttony is one of the seven deadly sins created by Christ. Too much of anything is never a good thing. If you are wrapped up in yourself, you leave no room for anything else good in your life. You cannot be self-absorbed. You must have an open mind and heart to let Jesus into your life. Strengthen your daily walk with Christ. Have the faith to call upon him when in need. You will soon gain the perspective on how to be capable to resolve all of the daily complications life has to offer. We all have these issues sometimes in our lives. With Jesus in our hearts, they become small. It is stifling to try to do this all by yourself.

Some people think they have no time for God. Some may think they are too smart and do not need God in their life. Others want something tangible. If they can't see it, they don't believe it. They need to remember that God has a perfect plan for us all. We must walk with him and keep him in our hearts for this plan to work. God will always be watching over us and forgiving us, as long as we believe.

CHAPTER 3

Overcoming Grief

In a way, death is a cycle of life. For every person who dies, one is replaced by a newborn life. Some feel this is God's way of population control. You see this in plant life and also in the lives of animals and humans. In the animal life cycle, it may be seen in the predatory instinct of others. This is considered the balance of life in the ecosystem and in the survival of the food chain. Natural death is the life cycle being naturally regenerated and replaced.

We are going to be discussing the death of a loved one and how it impacts your life and the others around you. We will go into great detail to sort out the emotions that are felt and what other people are going through when a personal loss of a loved one occurs.

> Where you die I will die, and there I will be buried. May the Lord deal with me, be it ever so severely, if anything but death separates you and me. (Ruth 1:17)

This may be the greatest statement ever made for complete salvation.

There are a lot of debatable opinions about death and how reactions are felt and dealt with. Some people are tremendously hurt by the death of a loved one. Other people are not affected as much and can go on as normal with their lives. For those who it deeply hurts, I offer this advice: in order to heal, you must make the choice that you are going to have closure. You must make the decision that you can and will get on with your life. No matter how it hurts, or how bad you feel about the situation, this was always God's plan, and you must accept this before any healing process can begin. Some people may alienate themselves from all others and just seem to coexist. This is not the plan God had for you in your life. You must refuse to let your emotions get the better of you. Ask someone for help in dealing with this situation. Talking to close friends, other family members, or even someone in general can help you see things that were holding you back and make you realize things that seemed unimportant at the time.

We must reach out to others who are grieving also. Some people get so overpowered by grief that they cannot function. Please step in and show these people genuine love and compassion.

I know you feel wounded. The most important thing to remember is that this is God's world. He created everything in all his timing and in his way.

In the cycle of life, we will all die at some time. We must accept that this is a fact of life, and we must move on. We must realize that this was God's plan for all involved. He created us to live, to serve him, and then to die. This is the cycle of life that he has chosen for all humankind. We must remember that in our darkest hour, God will never leave us, will never forsake us. He will always be with us, looking over our shoulder. The loneliness you feel can bring about alone time with God.

Our creation is of mercy. We should have mercy that he created us at all. If you want to solve deep problems that you feel, you sometimes have to dig deep into your soul to figure out how to deal with them and figure out the best way to heal faster. You cannot be reluctant to accept what is happening in your life.

> Teach us to number our days aright, that we may
> gain a heart of wisdom. (Psalm 90:12)

This teaches us that life is short, and that we do not use our hearts enough. We must be persistent in the grieving process. We must push forward and stand strong. Standing strong will build the strength in ourselves, our children, and our grandchildren. We must come together in prayer. Through this we will receive the right answer and be able to make the correct decision to better help us deal with our loss. If you have unmet needs, keep praying. If you have unfulfilled desires, keep praying. The answer you may receive may not be the one you wanted to hear, but it will be the right one as this is the answer that God has given you.

The death of a loved one can be heartbreaking to some people. I encourage you to be very supportive to others at the time of a lost loved one. This is a very critical response. If people are allowed to suppress this emotion, it only prolongs the grieving process. We must be passive listeners.

> For the grave cannot praise you, death cannot sing your praise; those who go down to the pit cannot hope for your faithfulness. (Isaiah 38:18)

It is said that when we are alive, we work for the Lord. When death comes, our work is done. In reality, everyone has a time to die, but in a loved one's heart, it is never the right time to pass.

In one instance of talking to people about how they dealt with the grief of a loved one, a young man told me how he felt when his grandmother passed away. He missed his "granny burgers." He said this is what he looked forward to every day when he went to stay with her during the summer while his parents worked during the day. He still remembers the way only she could make them and the way they tasted. These were better than any burger that could be bought. The best thing is that they were made by her for him with the care and love she had for him. When she passed away, he was affected by it greatly. His heart was saddened, but he was able to deal with it fairly easily because he was able to spend some alone time with her in her final days in the hospital. He was able to come to grips with the situation quickly, although he still has memories that sadden him some. He knew he could accept the loss because he has all the great memories that he looks back on from time to time. When this happens, he smiles and says, "That's my granny. You can't help but love her."

In another circumstance, a woman had lost her husband of fifty years. She told how it had been three years and she could still could not process the loss of her husband. She said that her emotions were so strong that she had a very hard time dealing with the issue. She said she had a lot of things going on inside of her heart and mind. She had feelings of shock, disbelief, and sorrow. Her recovery is questionable. To me it is a very sad loss. I offer these words to her. I hope this woman can rise above the circumstance and see that there is a light in tough times. If you can get through the valley and get to the top of the mountain, you can see the glory of God. I hope that she will realize that she has her fond memories, and that she will one day sit with her husband at the Lord's table.

> Precious in the sight of the Lord is the death of his Saints. (Psalm 116:15)

I had a conversation with a woman who has lost several loved ones. One in particular was a daughter whose life was cut short. She said that if not for having to stay busy with raising her granddaughter, she probably would have been unable to recover. She realized that this child needed her more than ever now and she could not let her down. This woman used the good memories and the love she felt for her granddaughter to help her overcome her loss. She still has some memories that haunt her. She said she still smells the perfume that her daughter wore every day before she went to work. She said that the first couple of years were the toughest, but she refused to let anything rob her of her joy and memories of this person.

> I tell you the truth, whoever hears my word and believes him who sent me has eternal life and will

not be condemned; he has crossed over from death to life. (John 5:24)

And to help demonstrate the willingness to forgive, I offer this.

The Lord our God is merciful and forgiving, even though we have rebelled against him. (Daniel 9:9)

We have to forgive to be forgiven.

Forgive us our debts, as we also have forgiven our debtors. (Matthew 6:12)

His forgiveness on our part is predicated on our forgiveness of others. To forgive someone who has hurt you or done something wrong to you means for you to forgive first. We must find a way to forgive all others for the wrongs they may do. This will help you move forward. You cannot hold a grudge or keep this feeling suppressed. If you do, it will always follow you and haunt you. Do not allow the feeling of hate or resentment to stay in your heart. Take the steps to move forward. You cannot afford to hold onto the scorn. Remember that you are saved by grace.

I would like to tell you about my own experiences with grieving for the loss of loved ones. I have a lot of immediate family members who have been taken from me at a young age. It has been very hard for me to deal with these situations knowing in my heart that they had a long and prosperous life still ahead of them. I have had to learn to overcome a lot of pain. I have struggled with deep sorrow in my heart and trying to get back on track and have a normal life. The passing of loved ones in my life has impacted me in such a way that I feel numb to hardships.

I have cried a lot of tears, and I have also been very angry. There were many times of uncertainty in my life. I did not know where I was going or which way to turn. I have had a lot of difficulty dealing with these issues. There was definitely a lot of uncertainty going on inside of me. I had feelings of shock, disbelief, and sorrow. I felt the tragedy was too much to bear at times. It brought out a lot of negative feelings toward myself and also toward others. When you allow yourself to fall down so low, you find yourself in a bottomless pit. Self-pity is an emotion that can very easily take over and bring you to your knees. During this, a person feels discouraged and can pass blame onto other people for his or her loss.

I wasted months, even years in excessive mourning. This was not healthy for me physically or mentally. I am here to tell you that the whole time, God was with me. I did not realize it at the time, but he was there looking over my shoulder. I was not going to go through anything alone. The day finally came when I was willing to accept what had happened. I finally made peace and accepted that death is a part of everyone's life. I learned a lot about myself and God. I prayed for God to give me the courage and strength to overcome my emotional instability. He gave me everything I needed and asked for. He saved me from a downward spiral that I may have never been able to recover from.

> I can do everything through him who gives me strength. (Philippians 4:13)

> Some sat in darkness and the deepest gloom,
> prisoners suffering in iron chains. (Psalm 107:10)

You can get through these tough times as long as you are walking with the Lord. Humans foolishly and futilely try to save themselves. You can't do it by yourself. It is impossible. You must seek help and the salvation of Christ. I have given all of my fears and problems that I have ever incurred to God, and he has always taken care of them. I had to realize that if God wanted my loved ones to be with me, they would still be here. I know they are in heaven, which is a great and wonderful place to be. I know that I will see them again one day. This why I want people to see that you can get through these times. It will be hard and you will have to give it everything you have.

> For I take no pleasure in the death of anyone, declares the sovereign Lord. Repent and live! (Ezekiel 18:32)

The Lord has no pleasure in the death of any soul. If someone you love is taken away from you, love from this person is taken from you. Always remember that our days on this earth are numbered. Life is a vapor and is always carried away with the wind. Make the best of all your opportunities, and always try to live life to the fullest, enjoying every minute of every day.

When you are going through a difficult time in your life, try not to build up any resentment. You must keep a positive attitude, and you will soon get through these times. Having a positive attitude about life has great benefits. It will allow you to have a good dynamic with other people. Having a good relationship with other people will help you overcome despair quickly and begin to move forward in your healing process. As humans we are given the great gift of being able to control our own destiny. Let someone know that you are struggling with bad and uncontrolled emotions. Do not let yourself shut down to the outside world. This will only magnify what is going on inside and will offer no hope. Always accept love and caring words from someone who is trying to help you overcome any obstacles that occur. They are your brothers in Christ and are only trying to help, as God commands us all to do. Try to stay focused on implementing the change that is needed to be successful in your transformation.

If you need to seek counsel, then do so. This will ultimately help you in the end. When you seek out others to help you in your time of need, this opens up other avenues and other opinions that may help you make the decisions needed to move in the right direction. Advice from others can be a great tool in overcoming your grief, as it opens up your mind and heart to other things that you may have never thought about or even taken the time to realize what has happened. Your health is the most important thing to take care of in the time of grief. You must take care of yourself, if not for you but for your family. They are just as important and can be the best help in your healing process. Remember that they need you too.

Some churches offer classes to help you overcome grief. Always check into what is available and offered to you. This can often be some of the best help you can receive from other people, as they sometimes know very little about the situation and can have an open mind and heart to the problems you are dealing with. You have to trust that God will get you through your troubles. Do not be impatient. Remember that he is always with you, whether you know it or not.

We as Christians have to relate to God as a friend or someone we have high regard for. It is the same relationship. You must let him know everything you are feeling and going through. Deepen your faith in him, and this will let him know that you are depending on him to get you through these trials and tribulations. Remember not to be impatient. All will be done in God's timing. Rest can be an act of faith. He will fix it in his own time. You must be patient and wait for the right time to come. You will know when he has set this into motion, and then you can properly process the results he has given you. Most people need help dealing with issues. They usually will not ask for it. They feel too proud to ask for it. They may feel like they are imposing on others, for whatever reason. Just ask for it; the help you may need is out there somewhere. It may even be closer than you think. Remember that God created us and he is going to be there for us.

> Therefore we are always confident and know that as long as we are at home in the body we are away from the Lord. We live by faith, not by sight. We are confident, I say, and would prefer to be away from the body and at home with the Lord. (2 Corinthians 5:6–8)

That is the sum of all things. It is a guarantee that we will be with the Lord forever. It is our faith that controls us, not our sight. The body you are in now is only temporary. You should not be afraid of death. It is a right given to you by God, for the passage into heaven. Knowing all of this should help you get through all of your troubles and pin. You know in your heart where you and your loved ones are going to be in their future life. Praise this and them,

Believing in the Cross

knowing there is a plan for them given by God. Knowing all of this certainly gives me the strength I need to carry on.

I feel like in my heart there is no question that it is my duty to help other people overcome their grief. I want them to be able to have an unending peace within their lives, which can only come from our Lord, Jesus Christ. From my heart, I beg for all to ask God for grace, mercy, and peace. He will give it to you. We all have a purpose in life. We must find out what it is and use it to help out others. God cares about everything in our lives. He is always inside of us, waiting to be called upon. We can't grasp all of his works with our minds. This can only be dome with our hearts. We sometimes get absentminded and forget what he does for us on a daily basis. Always remember that he is there, waiting to be called upon.

I am going to tell you how I got through everything that went on in my life and how I deal with my life on a daily basis.

God is our shepherd, and we are his sheep. God wants to be involved in everything in our lives. I therefore include him in everything. Through the good days, through the bad days, through the good times and the bad times, he is always included in my life. The Holy Spirit lives inside me. He gives me the sound advice and comforting heart that I desire. He taught me in the tough times, which sometimes overwhelm me, that it is he who is shadowing me and teaching me to be strong. Even though I have flaws, as we all do, he still loves me and understands me. I came to him as a child, and he has taken care of me ever since. I feel that I will never be a burden to him. It is Satan who tells me I am no good. I will never give up. I will always serve God.

> Even though I walk through the valley of death, I will fear no evil, for you are with me; your rod and your staff; they comfort me. You prepare a table before me in the presence of my enemies. You anoint my head with oil; my cup overflows. Surely goodness and love will follow me all the days of my life, and I will dwell in the house of the Lord. (Psalm 23:4–6)

I truly believe our Lord does all of this for us. It gives me strength. I am privileged to know that I have him in my heart and also in my life. So if you are grieving the loss of a loved one, always remember that there is always a place set for them at a table in heaven. You must carry on. Do not take your eyes off of Jesus for a second. Always follow his ways, and you will see his plan for you and your loved ones. You must keep growing in Christ. You will experience pains, just like a runner will. Do not let that stop you from pressing on. Our citizenship is in heaven, so rejoice, and rejoice in the Lord.

> In that day you will no longer ask me anything. I tell you the truth, my father will give you whatever you ask in my name. (John 16:23)

I am so glad you have taken the time to read this book. The most important thing I want you to remember is that even if we die, it is the plan that has been set forth by God. Do not be afraid of anything. Always look at what you have in front and inside of you. We all have a divine place that has been prepared for you and me.

Problems, emotions, and the loss of a precious loved one are some of the things you will have to overcome in your life. These problems can be dealt with easily with the help of others and your trust in God. You must always look ahead. Your soul is the most important matter at hand. It is more valuable than power, pride, and anything else in this world. Remember that and live by these thoughts and you will survive all that comes your way. We all have this power of resurrection inside of us. We must use it at all times.

> Jesus said to her, "I am the resurrection and the life. He who believes in me will live, even though he dies. And whoever lives and believes in me will never die. Do you believe this?" (John 11:25–26)

We all have this resurrection power inside of us. We must use it.

CHAPTER 4

THE LIGHT IN YOUR LIFE

Doesn't it feel so good to be in the presence of the Lord our Savior? God is doing work in our hearts. Make sure you are ready for the spiritual connection with God and the acknowledgment of Christ. This will set the tone for all of your chance to help in the minister of people and shape all the events that you will occur throughout your lifetime.

Some like myself are slow to get to know the Spirit, but I am growing. One of my favorite prayers goes like this: "Dear God, I am so thankful for your Word. It is the truth. Your Word reveals your will and your purpose. I am beginning to get a better working knowledge of your plan for me. I ask you, Father, to continue to fill me with the knowledge of your will in all wisdom and spiritual understanding so I may walk in a mater worthy of you, being fruitful in every good work I do. I thank you for leading me by your Word and by your Spirit into prosperous living. In Jesus's name, amen."

Jesus proclaims that there is only one door. This opens the door for our relationship with the Father himself.

> And when he has brought out all his own, he goes on ahead of them, and his sheep follow him because they know his voice. (John 10:4)

We should all learn to know his voice and what it says. He will always say, "Yes, yes, yes." Jesus is the light in our life. When we accept Jesus Christ, we become the light of the world.

> The eye is the lamp of the body. If your eyes are good, your whole body will be full of light. (Matthew 6:22)

Our souls should be full of the light of Christ. We should glorify his name. Without Jesus in our lives, they would be worth nothing. We must spread the Lord's Word and tell of the good deeds he has done for our salvation.

> However, I consider my life worth nothing to me, if only I may finish the race and complete the task. The Lord Jesus has given me the task of testifying to the gospel of God's grace. (Acts 20:24)

We must get our minds around it. Whatever happens in your life, you must do the work of the Lord. Do it unto the Lord. We must be passionate about what matters most. I am accepted through his Word, through prayer, and little by little, he unfolds the plan he has for me.

God is the light of the world. We should walk with him wherever he goes. He is the Creator and the Sustainer. We need to get to the heart of the concept of his passion for his children. Ask yourself what God's plan is for you. Ask him to help you follow this plan that has been laid out for you. Praise him and worship him, and he will always follow you in life.

> Go and enjoy choice food and sweet drinks, and send some to those who have nothing prepared. This day is sacred to our Lord. Do not grieve, for the joy of the Lord, is your strength. (Nehemiah 8:10)

This is the joy that filled God's heart, which means strength and safety. When we follow this example, we too will experience the joy of the Lord. This too will be our strength and our safety. God will supply us with all of our needs. We need to keep our heads and eyes forward toward the way he wants us to go. We must have an active participation in all things set forth by our Lord Jesus Christ. He will give us joy in our hearts and minds. We first must humble ourselves under the mighty hand of God.

Some people think that Christians are almighty and can do no wrong. Be assured that this is not the case. They are broken, trying to do what is right. God expects us to rely on him. When we are broken and down and have nowhere to turn, that is when we are restored. When we are in this state, we tend to trust God even more. We should have a common interest and want to participate in godly things and acts even more.

> Then make my joy complete by being like-minded, having the same love being one in spirit and purpose. (Philippians 2:2)

We must have the love that God wants all of us to have. We must have the desire to do God's will. The joy and happiness that he gives will follow in the days to come. When we accept Jesus Christ as our Savior, our work is definitely cut out for us. It may be a difficult journey to take, but we must stay focused and follow this path that is set forth for us. We should want to take on this task with everything we have in our hearts. We must stay in sync with what he wants us to do. We must pray for him to guide us to do what he wishes for us and to follow his path. We must pray for understanding so we can understand why situations happen as they do.

> Jesus Christ is the same yesterday and today and forever. (Hebrews 13:8)

God will never change. He will remain the same throughout the end of time. We all have the Spirit of Truth inside of us. We should pray that he may drop the scales from our eyes, that we may see the truth. He is getting ready. We must prepare our hearts and believe. Just keep doing what you are doing. Work, occupy, and keep your eyes and faith in Christ. A lot of people think that life is hard. In truth it is. These people may long for heaven or may feel like they have no one to turn to for help. We must put God first; he will take care of the future. I don't care how bad the times are. Put him first in everything you do. Shake off the heavy burdens you carry. God said, "I will carry them for you." God is the one who carries us through the bad times. He died on the cross for us. He gave himself so we could have everything. Pray that he may cover your family in the blood of Christ.

> When anyone hears the message about the kingdom and does not understand it, the evil one comes and snatches away what was sown in his heart. This is the seed sown along the path. The one who receives the stone that fell in rocky places is the man who hears the word and at once receives it with joy. But since he has no root, he lasts only a short time. When trouble or persecution comes because of the word, he quickly falls away. The one who received the seed that fell among the thorns is the man who hears the word, but the worries of this life and the deceitfulness of wealth choke it, making it unfruitful. But the one who received the seed that fell on good soil is the man who hears the word and understands it. He produces a crop, yielding a hundred, sixty or thirty times what was sown. (Matthew 13:19–23)

That is a wonderful parable of the sower—God's way versus Satan's way. You have to have the desire to understand the power that has been given to you. You have to also want to believe in the power that has been given to you. If you have made a good start at dealing with the tribulations you seem to have fallen upon, stay with what has gotten you to this point. Do not give up. Hear the Word of God with eagerness. He will reward you with more understanding and Christian growth.

If I would have known that all I had to do was ask to receive the Holy Spirit, I would have done that a long time ago. I did not realize that it is a gift from God. It is never too late to begin your journey with Christ and receive this wonderful gift. Life is so much easier and clearer when you have a feeling of security and protection inside you. God is more concerned about what is in you than what you are going through or what situation you are in that he can't change. Early on God promises this gift to all his children. This is sometimes referred to as the gift of oil and the oil of power.

> You have exalted my horn like that of a wild ox,
> fine oils have been poured upon me. (Psalm 92:10)

You must minister to your spirit. This is a total commitment and impacts inner belief. We must encourage ourselves to strengthen our faith in the Lord Jesus Christ.

> The spirit of truth. The world cannot accept him,
> because it neither sees him nor knows him. But you
> know him, for he lives in you and will be in you.
> (John 14:17)

We must make Christ our Savior. For him to come in, only the believers can understand and know him. This will enable us to live a victorious life in the eyes of Christ.

> But the counselor, the Holy Spirit, whom the father will send in my name, will teach you all things and will remind you of everything I have said to you. (John 14:26)

The Holy Spirit will teach you the Word. When someone needs your help, you will know what to say and how to comfort the ones who are in an insecure emotional state. Because Christ died on the cross, he gave us that right. He gives us the power to help others and change their situations. He will give us more power as we grow in the ways of the Lord. You must lock his will into your heart and let him be your guide. In most cases where you find people who feel they are down and out, you will find Jesus. He is always looking and always helping. You must stay on your course and be real to his power. It is an amazing thing.

The Holy Spirit empowers us to look for things we cannot see. Look for all miracles and blessings. It is amazing how God works and all he has done for us. We are all one in Christ. We walk together. We are in this together, not alone. This is a journey. You must open your eyes and enjoy the ride.

> However as it is written: "No I has seen, no ear has heard, no mind has conceived what God has prepared for those who love him." But God has revealed it to us by his spirit. The spirit searches all things, even the deep things of God. (1 Corinthians 2:9–10)

The Holy Spirit deals directly with man. He reveals God to us so we may be able to have the mind of Christ. We experience the dependence on God and his contribution to help us in our lives. We do not want to fail him in any way. The moment that we look to something else or try to do it ourselves, that is when we need to restore our faith in the Holy Spirit.

> Therefore, there is now no condemnation for those who are in Christ Jesus, because through Christ Jesus, the law of the spirit of life set me free from the law of sin and death. (Romans 8:1–2)

When Jesus died on the cross, we died with him. His resurrection is ours. We have to have the strength to deal with sin. We will have victory with the Holy Spirit. The Holy Spirit will show us the truth, we will know it when it happens. The law of the spirit of Christ is the strongest. The law of sin and death proves that we need a Savior. We have to have this to atone for sin and overcome its power, to save our souls and be sanctified. We need the Holy Spirit to work through us, giving us our fruits of the spirit. There is a difference between religion and a relationship. There are many religions, and there is only one relationship with God. Stay as close to God as possible; this is your relationship. Ask the Lord to reveal all truth to you. The Holy Spirit will quicken your spirit.

This refers to us being baptized in his death, which speaks of the crucifixion. This will depend on one's personal strength and ability or great religious efforts in order to overcome sin. The Holy Spirit works exclusively with in the legal confines of the finished work of Christ. Our faith in that finished work, "the cross," guarantees the help of the Holy Spirit, which guarantees victory.

> For the law of the spirit of life in Christ Jesus, has
> made me free from the law of sin and death.

That which we are about to give is a law of God, devised by the Godhead in eternity past. In this we have the Holy Trinity, God the Father, Jesus his son, and the Holy Spirit. You must have these three entities to have the Holy Spirit present in your life. These, are the two most powerful laws in the universe. The law of the Spirit of life in Jesus Christ is far more powerful than the law of sin and death. This means that if the believer attempts to live for God by any manner other than faith in Christ and the cross, he or she is doomed to fail.

This is very important. Read it, and return to read it again. You must get it in your head and feel it in your heart. This is the only way to fight the sin that comes into your life, even into you. Without this you can never overcome all that comes your way.

Trust me, I have tried and failed miserably, time and time again. I have had to have restoration in my life. You must have the Holy Spirit to deal with iniquity. That is the beauty of Christ. He takes it all away, all of our sins, even the ones in our hearts that are so easily covered up or hidden from others. See how much truth there is in Christ. This feeling is a heartfelt sincerity that is divine intimacy and divine compassion. Experience the essence of what God gives us. It is free, though not cheap. We must be honest with ourselves to live a grace-filled life.

> On one occasion, while he was eating with them, he
> gave them this command: "do not leave Jerusalem,
> but wait for the gift my father promised, which you
> have heard me speak about." (Acts 1:4)

> But you will receive power when the Holy Spirit comes on you; and you will be my witnesses in Jerusalem, and in all Judea and Samaria, and to the ends of the earth. (Acts 1:8)

He promises us the "pouring out of my spirit." We must trust God with everything. This is the ultimate expression of faith. This promise of the Holy Spirit is his will. We must accept it with earnest religious hearts. We must be alert to spiritual needs around us. Be very thankful, and do not forget to thank him for this work of God that is worldwide and given to humanity. We must be reminded of God's faithfulness. We must also be reminded that with God in our hearts, failure is never final.

Emphasize a grace-filled life. You must know and understand that you need Christ to get through everyday activities in your life. If the relationships with the people you care about most in your life are failing, realize that this is the Enemy doing what he does best. He is causing an unresolved conflict in your life. This can only be resolved by bringing the issue to the front and asking for a renewing of the mind. This is an intense spiritual battle. It is not of circumstance; it is of unseen wicked evil forces. They will devour and ruin your relationships. Pierce the darkness with God's Word. He will always help you figure out the way.

> All of them were filled with the Holy Spirit and began to speak in other tongues as the spirit enabled them. Now they were staying in Jerusalem God-fearing Jews from every nation under heaven. (Acts 2:4–5)

Believing in the Cross

Ask to be filled with the Holy Spirit. The Lord never does anything by accident. If you believe and ask and have faith, you will have righteousness. Our Father always brings glory to God. We are in the infinite care of God. We should magnify God. He saved us, he delivers us, and he always forgives us.

> For the Holy Spirit will teach you at that time what
> you should say. (Luke 12:12)

The believer should always look to the Holy Spirit for guidance and spiritual resonance. This is very powerful. We must believe it, live it, and use it. Take others by the hand, help them, be there for them, and let them see Christ in you. For yourself, use this on a daily basis. You need this in your life and in your children's lives. Provide yourself with what you need to make yourself ready. Have a purpose that is bigger than yourself with great opportunity for personal application.

> Go ye therefore, and teach all nations, baptize them
> in the name of the Father, and of the Son, and of
> the Holy Spirit. (Matthew 28:19)

We believe because it is the Word of God. Ask the Lord to use you. Seek the place where you are in need at that time. In our hearts and also in our lives we must find a way to follow the man holding the water pitcher, as he will lead us to the Lord, Jesus Christ.

> But when he, the Spirit of Truth, comes he will
> guide you into all truth. He will not speak on his

own; he will speak only what he hears, and he will tell you what is yet to come. He will bring glory to me by taking from what is and making it known to you. (John 16:13-14)

CHAPTER 5

Faith

I can understand why we all find it hard to have faith in unseen events. It is just so easy to not realize that it is there. We have faith that a light switch will turn on, but we do not have faith that God will turn around a bad situation. It is natural for people not to believe in something they cannot see. Once we realize and put all things together, it makes sense. After all this we still keep going back to the same pattern of disbelief or second guessing and even wondering if what we are feeling is real.

I am here to tell you that one of the worst things a person can do to Jesus is to not have faith or lose his or her faith in Jesus Christ. We must place faith first as the foundation for our love of Jesus Christ. The manner in which our lives are with God will shape them forever. The righteousness of God is only gained by our faith in him.

The reason there is good in this world is because of God. Everything good in this world is placed there by God. You must focus your attention on the life events of God and what he has done for you. You cannot say to yourself that this is the life that has been chosen for you. You must realize that all the events in your life are changeable and can be made better. You must strongly consider how many times God has shown us the way. He does this in some form every day of our lives. This is done countless times; we just do not realize it.

God will not deviate from his plan for us, even if we have a lack of faith in him. Satan's attack is always delivered against faith, for if that fails, we all fail.

> For everyone born of God overcomes the world.
> This is the victory that has overcome the world,
> even our faith. (John 5:4)

Faith in Christ gives the Holy Spirit latitude to work within our lives. Having a solid fellowship with God can gain you obedience of your heart. God will work in your life in ways you can never imagine. He will also give you a better understanding of the Bible and the way his teachings work in our hearts and lives. You will be able to obey the Word of God and walk with him wherever he takes you. We must have a deep gratitude for what Jesus Christ did for us. It is absolute certainty to keep our faith in Jesus Christ alive in our hearts and our minds. Love your Lord, and love your neighbor as yourself. We must remember that a neighbor is anyone in need.

> If I have the spirit of prophecy, and can fathom all mysteries and all knowledge, and if I have a faith that can move mountains, but have not love, I am nothing to love one another is Gods greatest command. (1 Corinthians 13:2)

Having proper faith will help you accept the Lord as your Savior. There is more to it than just believing. You have to show the world that you care, and you must show compassion for all your brothers and sisters in Christ. You have to serve the Lord and must be willing to serve other people in the time of need.

> In the same way, faith by itself, if it is not accompanied by action, is dead. (James 2:17)

I believe Christians have a strong prayer life and strong faith. You can usually see this in the way that they live their lives.

> For in the gospel a righteousness from God is revealed, a righteousness that is by faith from first to last, just as it is written: "The righteousness will live by faith." (Romans 1:17)

If we live a life full of faith in our Lord Jesus Christ, the good things will follow. We should expect them to follow in ways we will not know or may not even understand at that moment. We just have to know mentally that they are going to happen. This is another step of faith that Christ wants us to acknowledge. We must know what his will is, and we must prove over and over that he is satisfied with our hearts, our minds, and our souls.

As our hearts change, the things we desired before also change. We trust in God as we also trust the Word. We know the truth, and we feel it in our hearts. When all this comes together as one, we will also show it as God wishes us to. God has a plan for our lives, and it does start with faith. We must remember that salvation is gained by having faith. Grace will function only on faith. Everything good comes to you by having faith. Faith comes to by the Word of God.

> Consequently faith comes from hearing the message, and the message is heard through the word of Christ. (Romans 10:17)

We must believe the Word of God. Righteousness is also received by faith. We must constantly be aware of what is going on and use the Lord as our partner in life. This should be done on a daily basis, even when all aspects of life seem to be going down the right path. This means day by day and every day. You must do this more now than ever. The grace of God will flow to the believer on an unending basis as long as we have faith in our Lord Jesus Christ.

Keeping the faith means we are either a servant of God or we are a slave of sin. We will be pulled to serve God if we keep believing and strengthen our faith in him. The Holy Spirit can accomplish his work in our lives. We just have to believe in him. Without faith, regarding sin, our situations will just get worse. We must go to God daily in our prayers and thoughts.

> I have been crucified with Christ and I no longer live, but Christ lives in me. The life I live in the

body, I live by faith in the Son of God, who loved me and gave himself for me. (Galatians 2:20)

The only way we can be saved is by Jesus dying on the cross for us.

As the foundation of all victory, Paul takes us back to where it all happened. I will have new life, not by my own strength and stability but by virtue of me dying with him on the cross and being raised with him in newness of life. My daily walk before God will keep me focused that the cross is ever and always the object of my faith. This is the only way I will be saved.

It is obvious that everything the Lord does is done on the basis of the believer exhibiting his or her faith in our Lord Jesus Christ. We have to embrace our spiritual belief. We must have a serious thought of his work in progress. This will be your source of wisdom. To have peace, you must direct you mind on the things you want to think about. Our minds are our minds and can only be controlled by us. Keep your mind clear and alert to everything. This may seem hard at times, but it will strengthen your faith in Christ.

To some people this may seem intricate. If we can learn to live out of our hearts instead of our heads, it is easier to function and make the right decisions to follow. In my heart I believe that if you live out of your head, you are telling yourself, "Give me some truth." The Holy Spirit will reveal things to you. This will be done in many ways, and you will know what they are when they happen. You must realize that you can do whatever it takes to keep this faith. Have the power to believe in it. Faith always takes a chance in life. Faith is determined to be all it can be.

For we walk by faith, not by sight. (2 Corinthians 5:7)

Life is a journey; it is faith that controls us on this journey.

I would like to learn just one thing from you: Did you receive the spirit by observing the law, or believing what you heard? (Galatians 3:2)

It is probably easier for a Christian who has had faith for a long time than a new Christian who is now coming to Christ for salvation. New Christians seem to be skeptical of the works of the Lord. They do not fully understand his works and what he actually sacrificed for us that day on the cross. These Christians will soon gain the knowledge and faith in Christ that everyone should have when they fully understand how he lives for us.

And for your sake I am glad I was not there, so that you may believe. But let us go to him. (John 11:15)

Jesus wanted them to believe so that we may believe. Life is filled with difficulties. We must be devout, and we must be committed. Sometimes God waits for situation to go a certain way before he steps in and reveals it to us. Rather than solving our problems, he makes us work to solve them ourselves. This will be done in his time and in his way. By doing this, he will draw us closer to him in our hearts and our minds. He will never abandon us. It may be hard for us to get through the trials we face, but he will reveal himself when we need him more than ever. He will take our relationships to a new level that we have never seen. We must embrace the suffering. We also must suffer, to overcome whatever is keeping us from moving on. This is a fact that took me a long time to realize. I now want you to realize that this must happen before you can move forward.

Anyone can be a Christian. You must first go to the Lord in your thoughts every day. You must also believe with all your heart that the blood of Jesus Christ is real. You must believe and feel it in your soul that everything that has been told and the prophecies that have been given are all true. If you do not believe in this or have any doubt, you must ask God to take control of your life.

> Therefore I tell you, whatever you ask for in prayer,
> believe it, and it will be yours. (Mark 11:24)

Our relationship with God is what the key is. He created all of us. He also created all of us different. No two people are alike. We all have different looks, talents, and attributes that set us apart from one another. Understand the depth of all of this. He purposely made all of us different from one another. God took into account that we all have different gifts to offer. Someone else will always be an influence in your life.

> It is written: "I believed; therefore I have spoken."
> With that same spirit of faith we also believe and
> therefore speak. Because we know that the one who
> raised the Lord Jesus from the dead will also raise us
> with Jesus and present us with you in his presence.
> (2 Corinthians 4:13–14)

We must believe in him. This will bring glory to God. We are not perfect as humans, but God will always see us as perfect as long as we believe in him. When we act out against our brothers or sisters or say or do things that we know in our hearts are wrong, the Holy Spirit that is living in us grieves. He loves us. He is there to comfort us, but when we act out, it hurts his feelings. How much of ourselves are we willing to give? We give our time and our service, but how far are we willing to go when it comes to obedience and sacrifice to our Lord?

> He is like a tree planted by streams of water which yields its fruit in season and whose leaf does not wither. (Psalm 1:3)

Everything Jesus does lives forever and is blessed. This is a feat that is truly beyond this world. The tree is the believers! This is awesome news for us. We must direct our prayer to God. This will manifest itself into great things throughout everything in your life. We pray the Word of God. It is power and life. He laid down his life for us. This should be enough to make you realize his sovereignty and love for us. We should show it to him also. You should pull all of these things together with your mind for this to be understood.

John 1:13 says, "Children born not of natural descent, nor of human decision or a husband's will, but born of God." We are born again of God. We are made alive.

> The wind blows wherever it pleases. You hear its sound, but you cannot tell where it comes from or where it is going. So it is with everyone born of the spirit. (John 3:8)

He first chose us, and then he chose to come into our hearts. This is an invitation for anyone who believes in Christ. This invitation is very miraculous. It cannot compare with any other. This will make us complete as Christians. This will make us be the person God wants us to be. Our relationship with our Father is perpetual. It will last forever. When we die, our bodies will rest and turn to dust. Our souls will be given passage into heaven. Our souls will never die, and neither will they be forgotten. To me, one of the most important desires one could have is to have a caring and loving soul.

Share his love, receive him, and share him with your brothers and sisters. God is of the supernatural, and he lives in me. God has a plan for your life. This plan is a great thing, because none are alike. We must remember that Satan does too. You must know your signs and tell Jesus when you see them. If you ever get separated from God in your life, you must find the way to get back on the path he has laid out for you.

CHAPTER 6

God's Promises

When you give your life to God and let him into your heart, you can feel the boldness. Through this the Enemy can also see your boldness. If the events in your life are off course, stand still and see your boldness and God's salvation for yourself.

God has given us wonderful promises. Here are a few that have already been fulfilled by him: the covenant of Abraham, the commitment of Israel, and covenant with David. This should give the believer a sense of commitment, a broader perspective on the life of Christ, and a distinctive identity.

> Come all you who are thirsty, come to the waters; and you who have no money, come buy and eat. Come buy wine and milk without money and without cost. (Isaiah 55:1)

There is a plentitude of grace in the Savior. We have God the Father, God the Son, and God the Holy Spirit. What more could we ask for? Is Jesus dying on the cross enough for us? I think it is. You have a promise that others do not have—the promise that God gives you, if you will stay and keep your faith. You will still be standing. He will lift you, restore you, and heal you. He will bring greatness into your life. I want to encourage you to be part of God's action team. He loves us unconditionally. We should do the same back to him.

This should cause you to think about the things that matter most to you. This is a remarkable journey that we are taking at this moment. It is very important to understand the time frame we are living in. Things may not always be what they seem. That is why it is important to constantly be focused on our Lord Jesus Christ. If all you can do is say, "Jesus," there is power in the name.

> Praise be to the Lord, who has given rest to his people of Israel just as he promised. Not one word has failed of all the good promises he gave through his servant Moses. May the Lord our God be with us as he was with our fathers; may he never leave us nor forsake us. (1 Kings 8:56–57)

This is good news to anyone who is listening. You must ask the Lord for vision. This will help in you in your realization of Christ and the things he has done for us. I am going to hold on to these promises, and hopefully you will too.

It is remarkable that even today God promises to always be with us in everything we do. We can trust that he will put us where we need to be in our hearts and lives. This will give us the unique opportunity to experience Christ and all he does for us. It gives us a supernatural peace and strength that can never be broken. We can rely on the Holy Spirit for guidance.

> For physical trainings is of some value, but godliness has value for all things, holding promise for both the present life, and the life to come. This is a trustworthy saying that deserves full acceptance. And for this we labor and strive that we have put our hope in the living God, who is the Savior of all men, and especially of those who believe. Command and teach these things. (1 Timothy 4:8–11)

We must devote ourselves to the body of Christ. We need this so that together we can be strong in the entirety of our life for Christ. We need to build our relationship and direct our attention to serving God and serving others. I for one believe that it is such a privilege to be one of his children. Perhaps experiencing God's presence should be how we respond to our presence of the Lord.

> But the ministry Jesus has received is as superior to theirs, as the covenant of which he is mediator is superior to the old one and it is founded on better promises. (Hebrews 8:6)

I may fail, you may fail, but that promise will not fail. God and man should have a relationship that will keep the heavens at peace.

> Through these he has given us his very great and precious promises, so that through them you may participate in the divine nature and escape the corruption in the world caused by evil desires. (2 Peter 1:4)

God holds the answer to every question and problem. When we become born again, this is implanted in the inner being of the believing sinner. It also presents the salvation of the sinner and sanctification of the saint. We must show responsibility as believers to see what is true and to have the courage to do so.

God knows what we need before we ever ask him for help. The best prayer can be found in the book of Matthew.

> This, then is how you should pray. [It is to be prayed in full confidence, so that the heavenly Father will hear and answer according to his will.] Our Father, who is in heaven, hallowed be your name [our prayer should be directed toward our heavenly Father, and not Christ or the Holy Spirit, as we reverence his name.] Your kingdom come, your will be done on earth as it is in Heaven. [It is believed that at the second coming of the Lord, the will of God will be carried out on earth beginning with the kingdom of age.] Give us today, our daily bread [We are to look to the Lord for nourishment, both natural and spiritual. It will come in the things that we receive

from him in his will.], and forgive us our debts, as we also have forgiven our debtors. [The word *debts* here refers to trespasses and sins against others. His forgiveness on our part relies on our forgiving others.] And lead us not into temptation, but deliver us from the evil one. For yours is the kingdom and the power and the glory forever, amen. For if you forgive men when they sin against you, your Heavenly Father will also forgive you. But if you do not forgive men and their sins, your Father will not forgive your sins. (Matthew 6:9–15)

We should pray expecting and knowing that God will answer our prayers as to his will. Our prayers should be directed at our Father in Heaven. God's will is always carried out. We are to see that the Lord will provide for and support us in our life. His forgiveness depends on our forgiveness toward other people. He helps us stay away from living in the flesh because we will surely fail. God knows the strength of every person. He also knows what each person can handle emotionally. This kingdom is God's kingdom. He is the King of Kings and the Lord of Lords. This is not Satan's world in the eyes of a Christian. God has the power to deliver through the cross. God does deserve all of the glory. This will never change. God will confirm the destruction of Satan. We must forgive other people for God to forgive us, and this is very important for a person's destiny.

We must have a prayer life. For God's will, we must all have faith in connection with our relationship. We must reach to the Lord for everything. When your relationship with the Lord is good and you definitely are a true believer, prayer life is the only way to overcome all. As humans we have strengths and weaknesses, emotions and struggles. We must place all of our trust in God. This is what he wants and needs from us. He wants to be our safety net. By letting God do this for us, we will get the most from our relationship with the Lord, Jesus Christ.

> Submit yourselves, to God. Resist the devil, and he will flee from you. Come near to God and he will come near to you. Wash your hands, you sinners, and purify your hearts, you double minded. Grieve, mourn and wail. Change your laughter to mourning and your joy to gloom. Humble yourselves before the Lord, and he will lift you up. (James 4:7–10)

God has a plan for all of us, and we constantly look to him and what he does for us. We must acknowledge every aspect of our lives. It is living a victorious life that Christ wants us to have. We must repent for the good and bad. We must humble ourselves before the Lord and honor his high regard for saving us. We must keep close to God. He will carry us through to the end. If we generate all of the positive efforts he has put through for us, we will be able to see the end.

> Therefore, since we are surrounded by such a great cloud of witnesses, let us throw off everything that hinders and the sin that so easily entangles, and let us run with perseverance, the race marked out for us. (Hebrews 12:1)

This refers to the saints who look forward to the coming promise. We understand that we can only do this through Jesus, and what he has done for us.

> And pray in the spirit on all occasions with all kinds of prayers and requests with this in mind, be alert and always keep on praying for all the saints. (Ephesians 6:18)

God will answer all of our prayers to his will and purpose. The Holy Spirit wants to do good things for us and good things in our lives. This ultimately can be attained through relying on God. We do not have the ability to do it ourselves. We will only fail if we try it alone. This is considered self-righteousness. It takes the spirit of Christ to make the changes in us that need be made.

> Pray without ceasing. Give thanks in all circumstances, for this is Gods will for you in Christ Jesus. (1 Thessalonians 5:17–18)

We should pray about everything. We should never stop giving thanks to the Lord. This is the will of God. We should be able to accept what is from the Lord and reject what is not. A natural response to prayer life should be, "God give me direction and wisdom." Communicate with his desire, and pray more. He wants to give you peace. We should have a significant time of the day for prayer. We must have the visibility, with no distractions to listen to God and hear what he has to say. This should be a solitary place. We need an effective prayer life, and we need to be serious about what we ask him for. We need to be very patient when waiting for his answer, as it will come in time—his time.

We should write all these things down. Whether we are talking, or listening, we need to let him know we are paying attention to what he has to say and do for us. God is teaching us something that is very important, not only for our lives but also to help others along their spiritual journey. Do not be overwhelmed. Praise God, thank him, and do not worry; he will take care of you. The peace that God gives us is worth all of the time you can give to him.

Make the time to spend with God. He is there; he is not silent. Respond to the invitation. It is a privilege to share the gospel of the Lord. You were chosen, and he loves you. This relationship requires attention and dedication. God will never ask us to do anything he is not willing to help us with. We should fulfill and accomplish our hearts on how to communicate with God. We should keep our mind-set, Christ in our minds, and our eternity in mind. You must have the desire to be alone in your time with God.

He is very generous. He wants us to be diligent in seeking his face every day. Have meditation of your heart, particularly with obedience. Sometimes God wants to talk to us about sins that need to be addressed. Sometimes God wants us to amend our relationships with other people. Sometimes he commands that we obey the Word. The result will be a lifestyle worthy of the Lord. Never stop learning, and take comfort in what God teaches you. This relationship is highly sophisticated. It has great benefits, and quite possibly the most inspiration that you will ever get.

> Be diligent in these matters; give yourself wholly to them, so that everyone may see your progress. (1 Timothy 4:15)

To absorb the call of God, you must consider all of your sources. You must see what God breathed out instead of what God breathed in. In order to speak, you have to breathe. Be a witness to the revelation of his power. Every word carries divine authority.

First Timothy 3:16 says, "Beyond all question, the mystery of godliness is great." He appeared in a body. He was vindicated by the Holy Spirit. He was then seen by the angels. Soon after he was preached among the nations, was believed on in the world, and was then taken up in glory. These are all the things that are resembled in the attributes of godliness.

This gives me inspiration. It has all the distinctions we need to have balance in making life-changing decisions. We must listen with open hearts and affirm deep down in our souls that this is the meaning of our lives. We all need to realize that God created us to live in this life and in eternity. The light will always displace the darkness. Human knowledge is nothing compared to spiritual wisdom.

This will change your whole perspective. Get it from your head to your heart. We have to keep our eyes fixed on Jesus. Here you will find your pathway to wholeness. We must kill pride and self-righteousness in our hearts. We should be preparing ourselves here in this life. Will it be easy? No, but it will be worth all of the effort you have put into it. You must find out who you are spiritually before you can ever try to understand where you belong. For me, I know God is in control of my life. I see it every day in the things he leads me to do. I ask for you to understand what is happening and see it for yourself.

CHAPTER 7

THE WILL OF GOD FOR YOUR LIFE

In this chapter we will sustain the momentum we have gained in our learning process. We are going to prepare ourselves for what is in store for our lives in the future. We have learned that God spoke everything into existence. We have learned that because of Adam and Eve, the fall of man occurred. This event allowed sin to be born and exist. Even though Jesus died on the cross and defeated Satan, he still tempts us daily.

Most Christians believe we are at the end of time, and therefore Satan is strong in his way and is making a last attempt to destroy everything he can. We know we are living in Revelations 3, so we know we are close to the kingdom of age. We have also learned that God created us in his own image. The same resurrection power that raised Jesus from the dead is inside of us. We have also learned that Christ and the Holy Spirit also live inside of us. Through this, we have that God created us to live here on this earth and in eternity.

In the last days, God will pour out his Spirit upon us. We will see miracles being done. The New Jerusalem is going to be centered over the existing Jerusalem, being the new heaven for us all. We will understand all of this and why this place has been chosen for us when we reach this point in our life and join our king in heaven.

I would like to share a few scriptures with you that I feel are important.

> The heavens declare the glory of God; the skies proclaim the work of his hands. Day after day they pour forth speech; night after night they display knowledge. There is no speech or language where their voice is not heard. (Psalm 19:1–3)

There is no excuse for man not to believe in God, for "the heavens declare the glory of God."

The material earth is the sphere in which the heavenly message operates within us all. It is the first step toward the acknowledgment of God and all that pertains to God, which leaves man without excuse.

> Blessed are the poor in spirit: for theirs is the kingdom of Heaven. Blessed are they who mourn: for they shall be comforted. Blessed are the meek: for they will inherit the earth. Blessed are those who hunger and thirst for righteousness: for they will be filled. Blessed are the merciful: for they will be shown mercy. Blessed are the pure in heart: for they will see God. Blessed are the peacemakers: for they will be called the sons of God. Blessed are they who are persecuted for righteousness: for theirs is the kingdom of Heaven. Blessed are you, when people insult you, and persecute you, and falsely say all kinds of evil against you because of me. Rejoice, and glad, because great is your reward in Heaven, for in the same way they persecuted the prophets who were before you. (Matthew 5:3–12)

The kingdom is now present spiritually but not yet physically. We grieve because of personal sinfulness. The Holy Spirit will do proper things for our lives and the proper things for us to survive in God's will. He will help us deal with the spiritual poverty that lives within us all. The kingdom age will be the kingdom of heaven. In this the saints will rule with Christ as our supreme lord. God's righteousness will be given upon faith but must be truly empty of all self-worth. To obtain mercy from God, we must show mercy to others. People who have received a new moral nature in regeneration will see him manifest himself in their lives.

Peacemakers pertain to those who have peace with God, which comes from having salvation. Those who operate from the realm of self-righteousness will persecute those who trust in God's righteousness. Having God's righteousness, which is solely in Christ, has the kingdom of heaven. Only Christ could say, "for my sake," for he is God; there is an offense to the cross.

The present inner result of one who is blessed in rejoicing. Self-righteousness persecuting righteousness is the guarantee of the possession of righteousness and the occasion for great joy. Our reward may not necessarily come while we are on this earth. God's way may bring persecution, and severely so, at times by both the world and the church.

What are we fearful of on earth? We should not fear anything. We should look forward to our journey to heaven. We should focus on the greatness of God. We should never focus on the problems that have been created in our minds and hearts. God has the power to make any problem better. Do not focus on the problem; focus on God himself and his works. Look for opportunities to grow in Christ. Remember that we are living on earth, living our lives to get ready for our kingdom in heaven.

> In the same way, the spirit helps us in our weakness. We do not know what we ought to pray for, but the spirit himself intercedes for us with groans that words cannot express. And he who searches our hearts knows the mind of the spirit intercedes for the saints in accordance with God's will. (Romans 8:26–27)

The will of God for our lives is in place. You will notice that things you desired before will slowly change into something else. He will transform our hearts. We may want a certain event to be one way, but God may want it to be done in another way. Be patient; it will be go the right way under God's will. God desires change in our lives. It will be done.

The best advice that can be given is to always follow your heart and where it leads you. That is God's will for your life. We must always love God, desire him, and follow him, as he will lead us down the right path. We must discover what desires God has put in place for us in our hearts. When we do all of this, we will understand who we are. We must take our thoughts seriously and consider that they may be compelled by God himself. This is not a feeling; it is a choice. We can enter into a stronger and deeper personal relationship with God, our Father. We can speak with boldness. We can count on God to do whatever he can do for us.

> If you believe, you will receive whatever you ask for in prayer. (Matthew 21:22)

Doing all things according to the will of God, with commitment, will make you realize your grace in God and yourself.

> Do not conform any longer to the pattern of this world, but be transformed by the renewing of your mind. Then you will be able to test and approve what Gods will is his good, pleasing and perfect will. (Romans 12:2)

We must think spiritually, which is obtained by faith, and see all of this working in our lives. If we submit ourselves when we have the personal desire to do well, we will have the kingdom of God. The things that we cannot do, Christ certainly can do them for us.

> Ask, and it will be given to you; seek and you will find; knock and the door will be opened to you. For everyone who asks receives; he who seeks finds; and to him who knocks, the door will be opened. (Matthew 7:7–8)

Your heart must be right. Ask yourself, "Who is in charge of my life now?" Christ can change a person from the inside out. When we decide that we are going to follow Christ, we should make a commitment to bring other people to Christ with us. We must have affection for Christ. This will keep our hearts and minds. Nothing compares to this. All the glory belongs to God, and that is the way it should always be. People who grow know this is key to guidance. This is the key to progress.

We have great encouragement to get toward God. Those of us who draw near to God in a way of duty will find God drawing to them in a way of mercy. We must have virtue, and knowledge, temperance, and patience will follow.

When we have an awareness of the presence of God, he will guide us. If we make ourselves available to God, he will use us in the will for our life. If we do this daily, we will keep the presence alive through prayer, meditation, reflection, relationships, and reading the Scriptures daily. Do not stop seeking the Lord. You must never stop loving him as well.

God's Word

God has done everything for us. No matter what happens, we must remember God did all of these things for us. Let the Spirit of Christ move you. Let it compel you in your motivations and thoughts.

> Let the word of Christ dwell in you richly as you teach and admonish one another with all wisdom, and as you sing psalms, hymns and spiritual songs with gratitude in your hearts to God. (Colossians 3:16)

Everything is to be done in the name of our Lord. We must embrace the Word of God. You give it power. We learn to fight our battles with the Word of God. Man himself cannot survive by the bread alone. We must have the Word of God in our lives. The Word of God is like nourishment for our lives. Every day we must take the time to spend it quietly, praying and reading the Word of God and his Scriptures. The progress should show in every aspect of your life. The results will be astounding, and people will be drawn to you. The Word of God should be a prominent part of your life and inside of your heart.

The Church and the Body of Christ

We need each other for help. We cannot do anything alone. It is sometimes a bad decision to try to go alone through life. We must walk with God in all of our endeavors. We always need one another. We need to help each other. We all have a need to belong to something great. A church is the perfect place to bond with people. We get practical teaching from our pastors. We must find our pathway to wholeness.

> The body is a unit though it is made up of many parts; and though all its parts are many, they form one body. (1 Corinthians 12:12)

Our Savior is one in multiplicity, as is the church. We get baptized into the body of Christ. We must all come in through the same way. Our talents and spiritual gifts shine when we are together rejoicing in the Lord. Every day we reiterate God's Word and find our steps in the direction he wants us to follow.

In the church we all have a common interest and a mutual and active participation in the things of God. We have spiritual growth and unity of mind and heart. We have interest in the affairs and welfare of different groups and individuals. We have Christian fellowship in the desire to please Christ. We have friendships in our fellowships that last a lifetime and that have a strong bond with accord.

> I myself am convinced, my brothers, that you yourselves are full of goodness, complete in knowledge and competent to instruct one another. (Romans 15:14)

Our ministers have such great knowledge of the Word. They are anointed, and they speak the truth. The Holy Spirit works through them for us to teach us the Word of God. Everything is through

Christ and what Christ has done for us at the cross. They give us direction through and by the Holy Spirit. In return, we have authentic worship. We have a function as a church, and we have a purpose as well. All of this flows from our hearts, spirits, souls, and bodies.

We have a personal, passionate relationship with Jesus Christ. We focus on our worship. We have a profound love and devotion that enlightens the mind and body. We reveal the true meaning of who we are and that we are truly servants of the lord. We come to worship with thanksgiving. We are prepared and have purpose to have opportunity to worship. We learn so much about ourselves. We also learn how to obey the truth. We ask the Lord if he is calling us to do something, or even show us what the meaning is. This is the key to fulfillment in Christ. The old becomes the new, and the broken becomes the whole.

> Therefore, if anyone is in Christ, he is a new creation; the old has gone, the new has come. All this is from God, who reconciled us to himself through Christ and gave us the ministry of reconciliation. (2 Corinthians 5:17–18)

This is very powerful. It makes me feel like even if I have nothing, in Christ I have everything. It is reassurance that I cannot be afraid of anything. I cannot be afraid to die and place my life in God's hands. There is no greater feeling than the presence of the Lord. Everything good comes from God; he is the perfect gift. This is what God is, and he will never change.

The Bible is the rule. The story of the Bible is the story of the cross. The Bible has the potential to do great things in our lives.

It teaches us to have hearts that want to receive the Word. It is a requirement to obey the Word of God as a Christian. It will bring great blessings. Proper faith will always produce proper works. Victory in everyday life and living must have the help and power of the Holy Spirit.

The Lord has done so much for me. I have a hopeful spirit of optimism. I know there will be times when I am to suffer, and I know this is for righteousness' sake. Meanwhile, I will continue to try to suffer in the flesh and stop any dependence on self-effort so I can depend totally on the Holy Spirit. If I conduct myself correctly, the Lord is glorified in my life. We all should emerge in Christ. We will proclaim the wonderful and beautiful simplicity of the gospel of Jesus Christ. We have peace with God in our hearts. This occupies our space and expresses our faith.

CHAPTER 8

Salvation, Restoration, Victory, and God's Way

Salvation is a free gift. The good in this is that we do not have to do anything to receive this wonderful gift. All we have to do is ask Jesus to come into our hearts. Calvary is the means of salvation.

Satan makes you question your salvation, and he also makes you doubt your salvation. You should be able to realize the confusion that is going on in your mind while Satan is trying to take control of your life.

We know that faith is realization of things hoped for but on the assurance that they will come. Salvation is in Christ alone. We must believe this in order to be saved. The cross lets us know we are not capable of doing it ourselves. Salvation is not in our performance; it is what Christ does in our lives. We are given a new life. The Christian embraces the cross in our salvation. In our worship we will find hope to overcome all, and we will also find a new life that is prosperous and joyful. The only way to the cross is through an abnegation of oneself and the forgiveness of sins.

We must stand still, cease the use of our own personal efforts, and trust the Lord completely. God promises that salvation guarantees total deliverance, total victory, development, and fulfillment within our lives, for now and eternity. If we trust in the Lord, we will have everlasting salvation. This will last and continue time after time and last age after age.

Jesus existed with the Father, even before this earth was created. He knew the plan from the beginning. Jesus Christ is the equal of God and equal of man. He came here for one purpose. This purpose was to absolve us of our sins. He knows our innermost thoughts and all of our feelings in our hearts. As our salvation, Christ has gone forth, and if we come to him and seek him, we will find what he has promised us from the beginning. He is love. He is the personification of all man. He is the salvation that will come and the righteousness that will be revealed. Jesus is salvation, and salvation is Jesus Christ himself. We must lift up Jesus Christ. We must celebrate him in our lives and thoughts. We must remember that he brought us salvation by giving his life for us on the cross.

People are saved by trusting in Christ and also the cross. Believers are sanctified by continuing to trust Christ and everything related to God and how he relates to humankind. The second coming will bring us all of the results of our salvation.

> Surely God is my salvation; I will trust and not be afraid. The Lord, the Lord is my strength and my song and he has become my salvation. With joy you will draw water from the wells of salvation. (Isaiah 12:2–3)

The wells of salvation speak of a constant, flowing, never-ending source of unfailing assurance, consolation, hope, and victory in our lives. This is so reassuring. We must realize that there is always hope, no matter what the circumstances are. This lets me know that someone loves me so much that he would take my place at Calvary. He loves me unconditionally, as I also do him. I will receive his love. I will take it in, and I will hold it very dear in my own heart. I thank and praise him for the sacrifice he has made for me and all my brothers and sisters. He commands us to practice constant obedience. He wants us to be mature and act like Christians. He wants us to think of others in all we do.

> For just as the sufferings of Christ flow over into our lives, so also through Christ our comfort overflows. If we are distressed, it is for your comfort, which produces in you a patient endurance of the same sufferings that we suffer. (2 Corinthians 1:5–6)

We suffer as Christ did in our own lives. We will also experience the glorious benefits that were given to us when he gave his life for us that day on the cross. If we trust in God, we will have deliverance from all.

Restoration: when we become Christians, we think, *Oh, this is great*, but what we don't know is our work is definitely cut out for us. When you give your life to Christ, he does expect you to act a certain way and carry yourself in a certain manner. At first it is difficult. As you grow as a person and your personal relationships grow into spiritual awareness, it becomes your way of life. We are all broken, living in the flesh of sin and self-will. It becomes hard for anybody to survive in this situation. The key to survival is to stay focused. Remember: when the Enemy attacks, you must say, "Jesus, Jesus, Jesus."

Jesus wants to restore us through the Holy Spirit, but we must meet God's conditions.

> Restore to me the joy of your salvation and grant me
> a willing spirit, to sustain me. (Psalm 51:12)

A clean heart, a willing spirit, and a steadfast will are given by the Holy Spirit. We worship the Lord in spirit and in truth, and the cross is that truth. Being restored means we accept God as our Savior. We repent of our sins, and we continue to walk with God and praise him daily.

Victory

We all struggle with everyday problems. We all have hidden issues we must tend to in our lives. Most of these issues are the struggle between the flesh and the spirit. If we stop depending on self-effort and start depending on the Holy Spirit to give us strength to keep moving forward, we will have victory in our future.

> So I say, live by the Spirit, and you will not gratify the desires of the sinful nature. For the sinful nature desires what is contrary to the spirit, and the spirit what is contrary to the sinful nature. They are in conflict with each other, so that you do not do what you want. (Galatians 5:16–17)

We all have sin in our nature. We all have the consciousness of corrupt desires. It is the Holy Spirit who can subdue the flesh. If we believe and have faith, we can get rid of the old nature that we all possess and live holy lives as Christians.

The works of the flesh are adultery, fornication, uncleanness, lasciviousness, idolatry, witchcraft, hatred, variance, emulations, wrath, strife, heresies, envy, and murder.

If one is walking after the flesh, one or more of these sins will manifest themselves into one's life. The only way one can walk in perpetual victory is to understand that everything we receive from God comes to us by way of the cross. Consequently, the cross must always be the object of our faith. This being the case, the Holy Spirit, who works exclusively within the confines of the sacrifice of power on our behalf, will enable us to live our lives with him.

The Holy Spirit operates salvation, and he operates sanctification. Both are realized on the principle of faith. We all must have personal strength and the ability, along with great religious effort, to overcome this sins that arise in our hearts.

God loves us with sovereignty. God overrules everything in our lives. Whenever the Spirit comes in it, this will reveal who the real you is. It will show in your actions and in your thoughts. We cannot arise to this pinnacle in life by ourselves. We must have Jesus Christ on our side. This will make you free as a person, and then you will have total victory in life. Only Jesus can set you free!

> For everyone born of God overcomes the world.
> This is the victory that has overcome the world,
> even our faith. (John 5:4)

If we are saved, there is nothing standing between us and the Lord. Total victory is putting on our glorified bodies after the trumpet sounds.

God will make a way for you. God's way is perfect. It will not fail you in anyway. God has a plan for us all. As we grow, God makes us and molds us as he sees fit for us to be. The desires we have change our hearts. These desires change when we realize what has happened in our lives. This greatly impacts what we do and how we help others. I have been through many trials and tribulations. I have recovered from all of them thus far, but I only did this by finding God and making him first in my heart and life.

When you have recovered in certain areas, it gives you the power to help others. What was meant for harm has become my greatest quality and asset. I believe this is the process. This is how God wants us to grow. I help people every day. This is the purpose God has given me. I am very thankful to have found my spiritual gift. It gives me great pleasure to be able to use it, and know that this is God's path for me to follow. It brings a sense of spiritual guidance and direction from Christ.

Believing in the Cross

> It is God who arms me with strength and makes my
> way perfect. (Psalm 18:32)

Stay focused, and stay close to God. He will teach you the path you must take.

> Delight yourself in the Lord and he will give you
> the desires of your heart. (Psalm 37:4)

When you are a servant for the Lord, he does reward you. I have seen it, I have lived it, and it is happening. This is a pleasant reward and a great promise that has been given.

> My son, give me your heart and let your eyes keep
> to my ways. (Proverbs 23:26)

This is very true. It happens all the time. You must give your heart to God, and you will be able to see what is going on in your life. He will make it possible for us to do what we need to get it done. We must have contrition in our hearts. We all fall short at times. This is to be expected from us all. When we are able to see this, we can make the changes that need to be made and correct out shortfalls. We can then come closer to the person God wants us to be.

> Jesus answered, "I am the way and the truth and
> the life. No one comes to the Father except through
> me." (John 14:6)

This is who Jesus is. This is what he has done for us. We must learn to know him spiritually. We need to see him for who he truly is. Look at yourself and see how amazing it is. You must see how he created us. We must see how our hearts and minds work. This wonderful happening can only be God. We must look outside of the box and see the great works of God, our Father.

Seeing God's Splendor

When we realize what the Lord Jesus has done for us, we must give him all the glory and praise we can. We must thank him and truly worship him for the sacrifices that were made on that day for us. We must ask him to use us to do the good in the world for the people we may affect. We must go out and spread the word about Jesus and how he sacrificed everything for us. This was done for the love that he felt for us and for the people who believe in him.

When you look toward heaven, you must think of all the things that are magnificent that were given to us by our Lord. In order to be made free, we must believe in Jesus Christ. Our physical bodies are not permanent. Our glorified bodies are created by God and will last forever. We fear the Lord. What we do in our lives, we do before him, seeking to have his leading, his guidance, and his approval. It is so much easier to give your life to Christ than to try to do things by yourself. In this, I literally mean "self" because that is the key to this lesson. You must lose yourself and let Christ take over your life.

> Here I am! I stand at the door and knock, if anyone hears my voice and opens the door, I will come in and eat with him, and he will eat with me. (Revelation 3:20)

Paul had put himself entirely in the hands of the Lord. His life belonged to the lord. His message was to follow Jesus Christ and teach his ways. He himself knew the sacrifices that were made on that day on the cross when Jesus was crucified. This should help us to understand how deep some emotions run when we experience a life filled with Jesus Christ. As we learn more and understand the Word of God, his will for our lives, and the way of God, we must remember that no matter what happens or how negative things may be, we are to never stop giving thanks to the Lord.

If you are at a stumbling block in your life, or if you are confused, or cannot figure out what is going on, just ask yourself these few questions. What would Jesus do? Will my actions please God? This will help you understand the right decision that is best for you. You must remember that faith is the key that unlocks the door. If you are at a standstill, what do you have to lose? You must take the leap and accept Jesus into your life.

You can only gain knowledge by experience. Knowledge is a vast and ever changing. You will never exhaust the ability of the mind to constantly gain and accept new things. It is important for us to see that we must follow the path that has been set out for us by God. We must also trust in this path and follow it even though it may not seem to be the right one at the time. It may seem easy to get sidetracked and think that there is an easier way, but there isn't. The path that has been set forth is straight and narrow. The starting block is the cross, and the ending point is Jesus. Our walk of faith is straight. Do not look to the left or right. You must always be focused on what is in front of you. Do not lose sight of the cross.

Every blessing we will ever have was paid for by Jesus. Our healing is found in Christ. Our deliverance is found in Christ. And last but least, our victorious living is found in Christ. If you do not have faith, it is impossible to please God. You must make sure that your faith is anchored by the correct object of faith. There is no substitute for faith. Sometimes we may put more faith in ourselves than in others. It is the Holy Spirit that makes you realize that there is still too much "you" in everything you do. As humans, we will never understand the depth of self that lives inside of us.

The Holy Spirit is always chiseling away at the flesh. I am learning more and more every day. He is teaching me so much, and he will teach me a lot more before he is done. It is a never-ending cycle of life that I have chosen for myself. Everything I learn is so amazing. My relationship with the Father is believing in him. I am the one seeking him and his words of wisdom. Faith is what you have, and believing is what you do. I know that I must have fellowship in my life. I also know that I must have some time for prayer.

Each day I think of Jesus on the donkey. I think of the way he was smiling, being happy, and glowing. When I see these images in my mind, it brings me a joy that is a never-ending place. I find peace—a peace I can barely explain with words.

I want you to have this same feeling. I hope you will share this with your family and also with your friends. We must all spread the Word of God.

CHAPTER 9

JESUS CHRIST OUR SAVIOR

The life and story of Jesus is the greatest story of all. Jesus was conceived by decree of the Holy Spirit. Jesus came to Jordan to be baptized, and his ministry would soon begin for all the world to see. Jesus healed many people from diseases. He cured their injuries and also showed them that believing in the good attributes of life and believing in positive things will always make for a better way of life.

Jesus met many people throughout his journeys. These people became known as his disciples or the apostles. They were named Simon, who was called Peter, who he was closest to, who later betrayed him, and Andrew, who was Peter's brother. There were James and John, his brother. The other disciples were Philip, Bartholomew, Thomas, Matthew and James, the son of Alphaeus, and also Lebbaeus whose last name was Thaddaeus, and Simon the Canaanite. Last but not least there was Judas Iscariot, who was the last to betray Jesus Christ our Lord. Eleven of the disciples were Galileans, and Judas was a Judean.

Jesus did many wonderful things in his short life. He fed five thousand people with five loaves of bread and two fish. After the beheading of John the Baptist, Jesus set forth to a desert place in mourning of the loss of his friend. He had compassion for the people of this land and healed their sick. While he was there, he noticed that the people of this land were hungry both physically and spiritually. He said that the body of Christ is to be fed regarding the Word of God. He took the five loaves and two fish, and while looking up to heaven, he blessed and broke the loaves and gave them to his disciples and the multitude of people, and they did all eat.

Our Lord Jesus also walked on water on the Sea of Galilee, also known as the Sea of Life. Jesus demanded that his disciples get into a ship and travel to the other side of the sea. He soon went looking for them in the turbulent waters, knowing they were in trouble. In the wee hours of the night, Jesus found them as he was walking upon the sea. Where he walked, the waters became calm and serene. The disciples were afraid and troubled. They thought he was a spirit and cried out in fear. Jesus spoke to them, reassuring them to not be afraid. In disbelief, Peter called to Jesus and told him, "If it is you, then let me come out to the water also." Jesus extended his arm to Peter, and he soon came to the spot that Jesus was himself, walking on the water. After witnessing this, all of the disciples knew Jesus was the Messiah.

Jesus foretold of his death and resurrection. After walking on water, Jesus talked of how he would suffer many things and be crucified and be again raised on the third day. His death at Calvary would settle forever the sin debt.

Jesus was soon betrayed by Peter and Judas. He was arrested and had a trial, where the witness was false and unbelieving of him. Peter betrayed him by denying he knew who he was, and Judas betrayed him by telling the guards where he was. They were both in fear of being arrested themselves. Judas left the village in disbelief of what he had done. He met and traded the money that he had gotten for his betrayal for a rope. He soon hung himself from a tree. His faith and resolve for Christ had been lost due to what he had done. Judas committed suicide at the field of blood, also known as Potter's Field.

Jesus was taken and stripped of his clothes. The guards put a victor's crown of thorns upon his head. It is believed that the thorns on this crown were of six inches in length. They spat on him as they drug him through village. As he was dragged through town, he was beaten with leather straps, also known as the cat o' nine tails. It is said that he had fifty-three slashes over his body. His face was almost unrecognizable. His mother, Mary, had to watch all of this, knowing there was nothing that she could do to stop this torture of her beloved son.

They made him carry his own cross to Golgotha, where he would be crucified. They gave him vinegar and gall to drink. There were two thieves who were also crucified alongside him, one to his right and one to his left. Darkness fell over the land for three days.

During this tragic time, God hid his face from his Son. During this time Jesus feared the sin and penalty of humankind.

Jesus freely laid down his life for all Christians in this world. He did not die from his wounds. He died when the Holy Spirit told him to do so. The Holy Spirit felt that what he had suffered would be felt until time stands still by all Christians throughout the world. Jesus was buried in a clean, white linen cloth. His place of rest was in a secure tomb on the side of the mountain. This tomb was sealed and heavily guarded by guards of Pontius Pilate, for fear of the prophecy that Jesus would rise again. They also fear that the people would rise up and try to steal his body and make a martyr of him.

Mary Magdalene went to put spices on the tomb of Jesus Christ. There had been what was thought to be a great earthquake. She noticed that the huge stone in front of the tomb had been moved away from the entrance of the tomb. Christ had risen from the dead and left the tomb. Just before dawn, after all the soldiers had left to report what had happened, an angel told the disciples that Jesus had risen and was seeking all of them.

> Then Jesus said, "All authority in heaven and on earth has been given to me." (Matthew 28:18)

This was not given to him as the Son of God, for as God nothing can be added to him or taken from him. It is rather a power he has merited by his incarnation and his death on the cross at Calvary. This authority extends not only over men, but he also governs and protects the church. He was given the power to dispose human events. He can control minds and opinions of the heart. Last but least, the forces of heaven are also at his command, giving immortal life to all believers of Christ. The Holy Spirit is bestowed by him, and the angels are in his employ as ministry to the members of his body.

During his meeting with the disciples after his resurrection, he told the disciples they would receive power from the Holy Spirit, and then he was taken up to heaven.

Today there are a lot of different circumstances going on in this world. The most important thing to remember is when the Lord tells you something, you must listen to his words. We must always remember that God never does anything unless there is a meaning and purpose behind it. God does everything for a reason, and the Holy Spirit will reveal it to you when the time comes. We have to worship him in spirit and in truth. When you give your heart to Jesus, you will become a spirit in your own rights and ways. The key to heaven is prayer and loyalty to Jesus Christ. Praise will unlock the door.

You can feel the spirit inside of you. You must find it because it is the core of your heart and mind. This is the most vital part of yourself, of your being. Your soul should be the most important aspect of your life. Jesus loves all of his children, and he wants the connection with us. Let us all give it to him.

In closing, I would like to let everyone know that Jesus is my rose. He has the aroma of roses, and he is the rose of my heart.

Printed in the United States
By Bookmasters